"*For any entrepreneur who is looking for a proven blueprint for building a successful business, JK Harris has created what you need to find success. This book is packed with real-world examples which outline not only what to do, but also what NOT to do to succeed in an entrepreneurial business.*"
—**Will Brooks, The Brooks Group, Inc.**

"*Packed with no-nonsense lessons from an entrepreneur who built a two-person firm into the 800-pound guerrilla of its industry segment. I highly recommend anyone thinking about taking the entrepreneurial leap to read this book!*"
—**Brad Kurtz, CEO, Media Placement Group, Inc.**

"*JK Harris is right on the money with his knowledge of the challenges of business ownership and how most of us do NOT pinpoint the exact moment when the 'iron is hot.' This should become a textbook on the subject!*"
—**Rhonda Sanderson, Founder and President, Sanderson & Associates, the Publicity Specialists**

"*While many so called entrepreneurs dodge business problems with 'smoke and mirrors,' JK Harris addresses today's issues with sound logic reflected in a personal history of one man's mega success. The well worn pages of* Flashpoint *should be visible on the desk of every decision maker.*"
—**Don Abbott, Direct Response Television Marketing Expert, Abbot Productions, Inc.**

"In today's competitive environment, success is not guaranteed. The seven core business strategies in Flashpoint are based on JK Harris' 30 years experience in the trenches. If you want the facts from a veteran entrepreneur who tells it like it is, Flashpoint is the book for you. From my viewpoint as a marketing consultant, Flashpoint's key core strategy is to get to know your customer better."
—**C. Britt Beemer, Founder and CEO,
America's Research Group, Ltd.**

"Flashpoint couldn't be better timed—or, given America's perilous economic circumstances, better named. With legions of corporate refugees suddenly contemplating self-employment—by default if not by design—this book should turn into a must-read. Beyond all the baseline issues related to financing, market research, accounting, marketing, and the like, the book helps the would-be entrepreneur address an even more fundamental question: Do I have the right stuff to do this at all?"
—**Rob DeRocker, Senior Counselor,
Development Counsellors International**

flashpoint

SEVEN CORE STRATEGIES FOR RAPID-FIRE BUSINESS GROWTH

JK HARRIS

Founder and CEO, JK Harris & Company

EP
Entrepreneur Press

Jere L. Calmes, Publisher
Cover design: Desktop Miracles
Composition and production: Eliot House Productions

This publication is designed to provide accurate and authoritative information in regard to the subject matter covered. It is sold with the understanding that the publisher is not engaged in rendering legal, accounting, or other professional services. If legal advice or other expert assistance is required, the services of a competent professional person should be sought.

Library of Congress Cataloging-in-Publication Data

Harris, J.K.

Flashpoint seven core strategies for rapid-fire business growth/by J.K. Harris.

p. cm.

ISBN-13: 978-1-59918-364-0 (alk. paper)

ISBN-10: 1-59918-364-1

1. Management. 2. Strategic planning. 3. Corporations—Growth. 4. Success in business. I. Title.

HD31.H34547 2009

658.4'06—dc22   2009021583

Printed in Canada

13 12 11 10 09   10 9 8 7 6 5 4 3 2 1

With love to the two most important people in my life
and the reason I get up every morning:
my wife, Debbie,
and my daughter, Jordan.

Contents

Acknowledgments

Many thanks go to the individuals who took their valuable time to share their experience and knowledge with me over the past 30-plus years of my business career. While you'll see many of them mentioned by name in the pages of this book, there are many more who contributed to my success. You all know who you are, and I appreciate every one of you.

In a class of their own are a father and son who are no longer with us: Colonel James F. Risher, the founder of Carlisle Military School, and his son, Colonel William R. Risher, the headmaster. The Old Colonel's Sunday morning "Young Gentleman" lectures taught a scared 14-year-old boy the principles of honor and courage, that successful men face their greatest fears head-on and that they never, ever turn and run.

Colonel James F. Risher

The Young Colonel placed the responsibility and burden of leadership on a 16-year-old young man and taught him the most important lesson of life: Have compassion for those

Colonel William R. Risher

who make nearly fatal mistakes in judgment. The work of these two men changed

countless lives, and none more than mine. They have my eternal gratitude.

JK Harris

"No matter how busy you may think you are, you must find time for reading, or surrender yourself to self-chosen ignorance."

—*Confucious*

Preface

This isn't a book about how I became a millionaire and you can, too. That's not what I'm about. Companies have to make money to effectively carry out their missions, but there's so much more to being in business than profits.

Entrepreneurship isn't about getting rich. Most entrepreneurs make comfortable livings and some do, indeed, build significant wealth. But it's not about the money for most of them, and it's not about the money for me. It's about getting to the flashpoint, that time when your business ignites and you're on a nonstop trajectory toward growth, success, and making a positive impact on the world—or at least your corner of it.

That's what excites me: the flashpoint.

I've never been motivated by money for money's sake. Money is a tool that I use to take care of my family, fund a lifestyle I enjoy (although it's certainly not opulent), and build businesses that create jobs, deliver products and services the market wants and needs, and provide livelihoods for hundreds of people. Money also gives me the freedom to make choices that people who don't have money can't make. But I don't care about having money just to have it. You can't take it with you, and I don't plan to leave a lot of money to my heirs. I don't believe my heirs should be given anything for free; they should have to earn it—and they know how I feel. Things that you don't earn don't mean as much to you as the things you have to work for. The Sage of Omaha, Warren Buffet, agrees with me. He has given most of his money to the Bill and Melinda Gates Foundation and is leaving very little to his children. There are countless other entrepreneurs who have built large financial empires but don't plan to give a significant portion of the fruits of their labors to their kids because they want them to know the satisfaction of hard work and achieving their own goals.

My point is: Because I don't care about having a huge bank balance or massive net worth, and because I'm not building assets to leave inherited wealth behind, it's just not necessary for me to have more money than I need to live the lifestyle of my choice.

Yet though I'm not motivated by money, I'm absolutely passionate about business. In fact, I've been called a serial entrepreneur—and justifiably so, because I have started or owned 18 businesses and, as I write this, I'm developing still another. The thing about business is that companies succeed when they're profitable and fail when they're not. So to that extent, business is about money. But it's also about so much more.

During the course of my nearly four decades of working, mostly in my own companies but also for others, I've come to realize that there are seven core strategies which, if properly applied, can make any business successful and drive it toward rapid-fire growth. These are the strategies I've learned over the years, often through trial and error, that you can use to quickly build a business—regardless of your personal goals.

If you happen to be motivated by money, that's fine. These strategies will help you make money. If you're motivated by the need to learn new things, conquer new challenges, and make a difference in the world through your business, these strategies will help you do that as well.

In addition to sharing those strategies, this book is also my story of winning (and sometimes losing in order to win) in business. I truly am an old-fashioned American success story—I grew up in a modest family in rural South Carolina, was tossed out of public school and spent three years in military school, failed my first year in college and went on to put myself through undergraduate and graduate school, and have built businesses that have provided jobs for thousands of people. And I have a lot of years in front of me to keep doing the same thing. To me, that's the flashpoint—that's winning in business.

Winning doesn't necessarily mean that you're successful all the time in every endeavor. You won't always be successful. I've been a millionaire and a pauper three times. Circumstances change. Your operating environment changes. The market changes. I don't win every time. You won't either, but it's not because you're not a great player.

What counts is that you win more often than you lose, and that you win bigger than you lose. If you're tenacious and use the strategies I'm going to share with you, you'll do just that.

Being an entrepreneur is an adventure—it's the greatest ride you'll ever take. Don't worry about the prize at the end, just soak up the rewards that come along the way.

—JK (John) Harris

The Best Way to Read Flashpoint

Effective reading isn't a passive activity. To truly benefit from the time and money you've invested, read actively. Keep a pen and highlighter nearby; mark passages of special interest to you, and jot ideas in the margins. Write down ways you can use the strategies as you think of them so you don't forget. Dog-ear the pages, or use stick-on tabs so you can easily find your notes later.

Flashpoint: Seven Core Strategies for Rapid-Fire Business Growth is packed with valuable information—get the most out of it.

Flashpoint

noun

1. The lowest temperature at which the vapor of a combustible liquid can be made to ignite momentarily in air

2. A point at which someone or something bursts into significant action or creation

Figure Out What You Don't Know

Did you know that a Taser probe travels at a speed of more than 160 feet per second? And when it hits its target, it delivers an incapacitating electrical shock.

Today's business environment is a lot like a stun gun—challenging, unforgiving, and moving at an incredibly fast pace, with the ability to bring you to your knees in seconds. At the same time, the opportunities for entrepreneurs have never been greater. Corporate giants may still be the most visible business entities, but we have learned that, while size matters, bigger isn't necessarily better.

Of course, it's easy to start and run a business when the economy is booming. You can make a lot of mistakes and still come out on top—I know, because I've done just that. There's much less margin for error in a down economy—again, I know, because I've been through plenty of economic downturns in several different industries. The key to survival is to do things smart. That means you have to move quickly and precisely. You must be flexible, able to roll with the punches, get back on your feet immediately, and change your strategies when necessary. Most important, you need to hit your target with deadly accuracy, even when the target is moving.

There's nothing more exciting and rewarding for an entrepreneur than to build a business that meets a need in the marketplace and creates jobs for people, whether that business serves customers only in your town or around the world, whether it employs one person or thousands of people. Some entrepreneurs are motivated by the money they can make through their businesses and may even believe that the purpose of their venture is profit. Management guru Peter Drucker says, "The purpose of a business is to create a customer." He's right, of course, because customers generate the revenue that businesses must have to stay in business. But Drucker's statement doesn't go far enough. The purpose of a business is to also create jobs.

> *"I rarely regretted acting but often regretted not acting fast enough."*
> —Jack Welch

So while some entrepreneurs are motivated by the money, I believe most are more like me: I'm motivated by learning and doing new things while I meet a need in the market and create jobs that provide interesting work and decent livelihoods for my employees and their families. It really is about the journey, not the destination.

Sometimes It's Luck

The Roman philosopher Seneca said, "Luck is what happens when preparation meets opportunity."

Whether you have good luck or bad depends on how you respond to circumstances. The circumstances happen mostly by chance; how you react is what determines the impact of chance on you and your company. Extraordinarily successful people reach their achievements because they're smart, skilled, willing to work hard—and lucky enough to be in the right place at the right time. In discussing his book *Outliers: The Story of Success* (*outliers* is a scientific term that describes things or phenomena that lie outside normal experience), Malcolm Gladwell says, "You know how you hear someone say of Bill Gates or some rock star or some other outlier—'they're really smart' or 'they're really ambitious'? Well, I know lots of people who are really smart and really ambitious, and they aren't worth $60 billion. I think we vastly underestimate the extent to which success happens because of things the individual has nothing to do with." If John, Paul, George, and Ringo had been born 20 years earlier or later, would the Beatles have become one of the world's most commercially successful and critically acclaimed bands? If Donald Trump's father had been a school-teacher or a truck driver, would "The Donald" have grown up to be the celebrity billionaire businessman he is today? Of course, we don't know—and I'm not in any way disparaging the success of these tremendously accomplished individuals. Nor am I suggesting that because the circumstances under which they've operated can never be duplicated that others won't be able to achieve comparable results. What you accomplish in life is the result of a total package of who you are, how hard you're willing to work, and circumstances beyond your control.

Sometimes it just happens that everything aligns perfectly and things will go well, no matter what you do, like when I owned a mechanical construction business in South Carolina at the time Hurricane Hugo hit. Because of the incredible amount of damage the storm caused, I had more business than I could handle. Sometimes the reverse will happen, like when that same mechanical construction company collapsed as a result of the military base closures and recession in the early 1990s. I tried to keep the company afloat, but there just wasn't enough business to do it.

Most of the time, your success is a direct result of how well-prepared you are and what action you choose to take. I'll take preparation over chance any day—and one of the first steps in preparing for success is to understand what you don't know.

People like Bill Gates, Paul Allen, Steve Jobs, Larry Ellison, Oprah Winfrey, Richard Branson, Anita Roddick, Harvey Mackay, and others happened to have been born at the right time and landed in the right place to build their companies. But what separated those particular individuals from everybody else who was born at that time and grew up in the same environment? They saw the opportunity, figured out what they didn't know and needed to learn, and put forth the necessary effort and time to master their chosen professions. And that's how they became successful.

Only a few individuals will actually seize the opportunity that's presented by the circumstances. You can get lucky—but it won't matter if you don't have the vision to recognize it and are willing to do what it takes to take advantage of your luck.

An Interesting Journey

When I look back on my youth, I'm well aware that my life could have turned out very differently. By the time I reached my teens, I was well on my way to becoming a juvenile delinquent, the boy that nice girls weren't allowed to date, often in some sort of trouble, hanging out with the wrong people. In fact, of my three closest friends from my early teens, only one is still alive—and coincidentally, his wife now works for JK Harris & Company. I didn't know who her husband was until I met him at a company party; we hadn't seen each other in more than 30 years. But he and I turned our lives around; the other two didn't, and they paid a horrible price.

I grew up on a dairy farm in South Carolina. I was smart and easily bored, which was the perfect recipe for trouble for a kid. In March 1968, I was expelled from the public school system. I got a summer job driving a delivery truck for a dry cleaner, then in August, my parents enrolled me in Carlisle Military School in Bamberg, South Carolina.

My father was a strong man, but I remember he had tears in his eyes that hot, muggy summer morning that he left me at Guild's Hall, a large, two-story brick dormitory. He knew what a turning point this was going to be for me. His mother had taken him to a Marine Corps recruiting station when he was 17 and signed for him to enlist (he ended up fighting in the South Pacific during World War II) to get him away from his abusive father. So my father was very familiar with the military life; he knew I had a lot to learn and the lessons weren't likely to be easy—but they were essential. For many boys at that time, military school was just one step removed from reform school. Most of my classmates were like me—troubled kids in desperate need of something or someone that could get them on the right track. The school's mission, articulated by its headmaster, Colonel James F. Risher, is to "accept young men of unfulfilled promise and lead them to a future of success."

Carlisle certainly met its mission with me. When I first arrived, I was defiant and ready to fight anybody. Punishment for rule infractions was to spend time walking the "bull ring"—not a pleasant thing in the oppressive South Carolina heat and humidity. But I spent virtually every free minute for the first eight weeks walking the bull ring with a 30-pound World War II rifle on my shoulder.

It didn't take me long to wise up. I realized that all the cadets out on the bull ring were the losers. The smart guys were sitting back in the cool buildings. I decided that's where I wanted to be. And when I stopped rebelling, I began to understand what this environment could teach me. At the end of my first year, I was promoted

> *"Just because you make a mistake doesn't mean you are a mistake."*
> —Georgette Mosbacher

to First Sergeant, a rank I held for my second year. When I came back for my senior year, it was as the Company Commander. The faculty made the decisions on who would be promoted to which rank. At the time, I didn't completely comprehend this, but as I look back, it's clear that they saw how much maturing and learning I did in a relatively short time. To paraphrase a popular book title, "All I ever needed to know, I learned in military school."

Not Quite Ready for Prime Time

This isn't to say that I came out of Carlisle an angel destined to live a perfect life—far from it. I graduated from military school in June 1971 and started at the College of Charleston in the fall. I majored in partying. In the first semester, I went to each class exactly three times, and still managed to get acceptable grades—probably due in large part to the quality of the education I had received at Carlisle. In the second semester, I wasn't so lucky. I followed the same attendance pattern, but this time I failed three courses and barely passed the other two. I couldn't go back to school, so I got a job driving a Pepsi-Cola delivery truck. I spent four months delivering cases of soft drinks to stores in the summer. I worked in oppressive heat, hauling heavy cases and sorting empty bottles in the backs of stores with roaches and rats crawling around.

Even though I worked with some great people, it was a hot, dirty, difficult job, and it woke me up to reality. That job convinced me that I never wanted to do physical labor, that I wanted to work with my head. At the same time, I realized that just "wanting" wasn't enough. If I didn't get an education, I'd be doing jobs just like that one for the rest of my life. I'd gotten a taste of leadership at Carlisle, of being at the top, and I didn't like being back on the bottom rung of the ladder without much chance of climbing up.

I convinced my father that I'd learned my lesson and was ready to go back to college and do it right. He let me move back home, and my mother used her teaching connections to get me into the

University of South Carolina at Columbia that fall on a special probation status. I saved every penny I made from that delivery job to pay my tuition and my initial living expenses—I wasn't exactly scholarship material—until I found a job.

The job I found was as a night shift clerk at Owen Steel Company Inc., a steel rebar mill. It was one of the best jobs I'd ever have. For three years, I worked at Owen Steel full time and went to school full time. I made straight A's and, in spite of my dismal first two semesters in Charleston, still managed to graduate *cum laude*.

My job at Owen Steel taught me some interesting things about myself and about business and management. One is that I'm basically a lazy person, and there's absolutely nothing wrong with that. There are two kinds of lazy people—ones like me, who are always looking for the easiest, most efficient way to get things done, but who do indeed, get the job done and do it well, and ones who just don't care if the work gets done or not. Another thing I learned is when you're fortunate enough to get employees who demonstrate my kind of laziness, take advantage of it because they'll increase the productivity of your organization.

As the night shift clerk, I was responsible for generating the production reports from the first shift for that day. At that time, the company wasn't computerized, so I had to gather all the information, make all the calculations, and prepare the reports. I also functioned as the night office manager, which basically meant being available if something unusual happened. For example, there were several occasions over the years that I drove injured workers to the emergency room. In the beginning, it took me at least six hours to do those production reports. Within a month, I was knocking them out in two hours. I felt guilty taking a full day's pay for just a couple of hours of work, so I went to my boss and told him how much time it was really taking me to do the job.

My shift started in the midafternoon and I worked through the evening. My boss told me to make it look like I was working

The Business of Ethics

Business as usual is, unfortunately, not always business at its best—especially when it comes to ethics. I believe there are two driving forces behind virtually all unethical business behavior: greed and the need to go along to get along.

My first business was an asphalt paving company I bought in 1979. I learned some important lessons about things like collusion, bid-rigging, and making choices. There were more lessons to be learned during the years I worked at and owned car dealerships. I'll be sharing those stories throughout this book, but for now, I'll just say that the difference between right and wrong is usually obvious, but the decision isn't always easy.

Every industry, every business is fraught with ethical choices. This is part of the circumstances you have to learn to deal with in life. In my early years, I made some wrong decisions. Today, I don't waste time regretting them, but I'm not going to repeat them. I will not compromise my ideals and beliefs for any business or any amount of money. And I recommend that you take the same position. You might not make as much money, your company might not get as big, but you can still be profitable and grow—and you'll be able to sleep at night, soundly, in your own bed instead of a prison cell. To me, that's worth everything.

until everyone else left the office and the only people left in the facility were the plant workers, then to spend the rest of my shift—after I'd completed the reports—studying. He told me if I made straight A's, it would be worth it for him. So that's what I did.

As great as that job was, it also reinforced what I'd learned while driving the Pepsi-Cola delivery truck: I didn't want to do manual labor, I wanted to work with my mind, and I much preferred being in a leadership position. The key difference between the guys in the mill, the ones doing hard physical labor in challenging conditions, and the guys in the office, who wore ties and worked in a comfortable, air-conditioned environment, was education. It wasn't intelligence, it was knowledge.

Moving On

I graduated with a degree in history and political science, got married, and went on to earn a Master of Accountancy in 15 months while my wife worked and supported us. Then I took a job as a staff accountant at Haskins & Sells, CPAs (now Deloitte Touche Tohmatsu) in Charlotte, North Carolina. I quickly learned that as much as I had enjoyed learning the theoretical part of accounting in school, I wasn't by nature an accountant. I found doing the actual work of accountancy boring, boring, boring. But I stuck it out at Haskins & Sells for a little more than a year and got my CPA certificate.

To keep my mind challenged during that time, I learned to fly a plane, and my wife and I built our first house. I designed it, taught myself the fundamentals of drafting in order to draw plans for residential structures, then acted as the general contractor (which you can do without a license if you're building your own house). Through that experience, I recognized my love of building things, not necessarily hammering the nails but making it all happen, turning a concept into a concrete thing you could touch and use.

I wanted to be in business for myself, but I realized I lacked knowledge and experience in a key area: I needed to learn how to sell. I was an expert in accounting, the language of business, but what really makes a company tick are the people who go out and sell. They make it all happen.

I left Haskins & Sells to take a position with Connecticut General Life Insurance Company, which at the time was the country's top producer of insurance for business buy-sell agreements. A buy-sell agreement is designed to protect the owners of closely held corporations and partnerships in the event of the death or disability of one of the owners. Typically, the buy-sell agreement stipulates that the surviving owner(s) or partner(s) purchase the share(s) belonging to the deceased or disabled owner or partner, and that purchase is funded by insurance. Calculating the value of the company and the appropriate amount of coverage is a complicated process. Connecticut General needed a CPA to assist their insurance sales representatives as they put together buy-sell life insurance policies for businesses.

This was an excellent training ground for someone like me who didn't want to actually do the selling but wanted to learn how it worked. And even though I didn't want to be a full-time salesperson, there have been plenty of opportunities over the years for me to use the sales skills I learned watching the Connecticut General reps work. In the early days of JK Harris & Company, I did all the sales until I could afford to hire sales reps. During my years in the automobile industry, I spent some time managing sales teams and I couldn't have done it had I not understood what they needed to do. I have used selling skills when dealing with lenders and investors—sure, I could have just showed them a stack of financial statements and hoped they would trust me with their money, but that wouldn't have been nearly as effective as being able to apply selling skills to my presentations. I even use selling skills when dealing with my employees—yes, I could just lay down the law and tell them what to do, but it's far more effective to use selling and persuasion techniques to get them to make it their decision.

> "We succeed in enterprises which demand the positive qualities we possess, but we excel in those which can also make use of our defects."
> —Alexis De Tocqueville

At Connecticut General, I spent my days with true sales professionals, some of them 30-year veterans, who knew how to identify needs, develop solutions, handle objections, and close the sale. One of the most educational deals I saw was the sale of a $60 million (yes, that's 60 million, no typo there) life insurance policy to the family that owned Coca-Cola Bottling in Charlotte, North Carolina. Think about your own life insurance premiums, and you'll realize what a huge transaction that was and how skilled the sales rep had to be to close it.

After six months, I decided my sales education was complete. I had learned enough to be in business for myself. So I went shopping for a business to buy.

And then I learned how much I still didn't know.

You're Not As Smart As You Think You Are

Once you admit that you aren't as smart as you think you are—or as you want other people to believe—you're going to get a lot smarter.

The two best ways to get smarter are to

1. study everything you can get your hands on about your industry, and
2. tap into the knowledge of the people who understand your industry and who have information you can use.

Sometimes you have to pay for the information; other times you can get it for free. What it costs you doesn't really matter, because I can assure you that the cost of not knowing is far greater than whatever you'll spend on learning.

The more you know, the easier it will be for you to determine what's good, valid information and what isn't. That's why your information needs to be from a variety of sources. When your sources agree, that's a sign that you can probably (but not always) trust what they're saying. When they disagree, you need to do more research.

I'm fortunate because I love to read. When I was a youngster, my mother taught me not only to read fast but to comprehend what I was reading as well. So whenever I wanted to know something, the first place I looked was a library or bookstore. Today, of course, I also search the internet—but I still love libraries and bookstores, and I end up buying books because they have information that I want. I also know not to trust everything I read on the internet. Something that I consider when I'm reading a book is the sources the author used. Reading gives me the foundation I need for any subject, whether I'm learning for business or personal reasons. If you're not a strong reader, I recommend investing in some adult education classes that will help you develop your reading and comprehension skills. And be a discriminating reader— just because it's written down doesn't make it true.

Of course, reading is not the only way to learn. You can take classes, listen to and watch educational broadcast programs, and spend time around people who know what you don't. Trade and professional associations are great resources for that, because they offer opportunities for you to network with others who may have a different experience base than you.

When I purchase an existing company, I'm sure I can do a better job running it than whomever I'm buying it from; otherwise I probably wouldn't be interested in buying it. If I don't think I can improve and grow the company, there's no point in taking it over. At the same time, I'm well aware that the selling owner knows a whole lot that I'm going to need to know. I may believe I'm smarter than he is, but he knows more about his business than I do. That's why I like to contract with the selling owner to stick around for at least a year, sometimes longer, to help run the company during the transition. That worked great for me when I bought my first company, an asphalt paving business, in 1979. It wasn't possible when I bought a bankrupt mechanical construction business a decade later—the reason the business was bankrupt was because the owner had been robbing it blind, and I later found out that this wasn't the first time this guy had put a business under on purpose. But he had some good people working for him—people who knew more about the business than I did—and they were willing to stay on with me and help me turn the company around.

I think entrepreneurs tend to be above average in intelligence, and I know I'm a smart guy. But I also know that I don't know it all. You don't, either. In his book *Outliers*, Malcom Gladwell confirmed that. He studied successful people and determined that they were not geniuses. The people he classified as outliers—that is, people who are considered outside what we think of as "normal"—had IQs of about 20 points above average to about 20 points below genius. These people didn't know everything and they knew it, but they also knew where to go for the information they needed.

When you know what you don't know, you're ideally positioned for growth and achievement.

Succeed Big, Fail Small

You're going to make mistakes—lots of them. And that's OK, because that's how you learn. Just take care to minimize the impact of those mistakes. Make your successes big and your failures small, and you'll always come out ahead.

I have used emotional direct response marketing in a number of businesses over the years. This is a type of marketing that solicits a very direct response that's driven by strong emotion from the consumer. The desired consumer response will typically be something like "call now" or "come in" to either make a purchase or get more information. The emotional drivers vary depending on the product or service, but they always have to be strong or the people on the receiving end of your marketing efforts won't be motivated to take action.

Figure Out What You Don't Know　　　　　　　　　　　　　　　**13**

One of the most important lessons I learned from direct response marketers is to test everything that you can possibly test. Never assume that any idea will work; always test it for proof. Certainly you should test any marketing strategy before you roll it out, but more than that, you should also test your other business operations and product ideas on a smaller scale before you move to a full-scale implementation.

Testing allows you to keep your failures small and make your successes big. Don't go out and blow your entire budget on one idea. Let's say you have three different marketing ideas and you're not sure which one will work the best. Your total budget for the year is $100,000. Instead of picking one of those ideas and taking a chance on spending your entire $100,000 budget, test all three with budgets of $10,000 each. When you're finished testing, you'll know which idea works the best, and you'll still have $70,000 left to spend on it. Or, let's say you only have one idea. Test it on a small scale anyway, because that will tell you whether or not it's going to work. If you spend $10,000 on the test and you're satisfied with results, great. But if you spend $10,000 and you aren't satisfied, you need to come up with another idea—and at least you've still got $90,000 left to spend.

> "[W]e are changed by what we read. Close that book, and you are not the same person anymore. Because of what you just read, your worldview—your understanding, your compassion for others, your ability to engage intelligently with others— has expanded a little. Books help us grow."
>
> —Pat Williams

You can apply the testing concept to other parts of your company, including product development, employee recognition and compensation, organizational structure, and general operations. I'm going to share a lot of great ideas with you in this book, but you shouldn't just blindly use them. Think about them carefully, figure out the best way to apply them, and then test before you implement.

If you test something that doesn't work and it fails, you didn't lose. You simply made an investment to find out whether you should do a larger implementation. You spent some money and the knowledge you gained was worth it.

Now, having said that, I must also say that you won't have time to test everything. Sometimes you'll have to go with your gut because you have to move quickly. Occasionally you'll choose to go with your gut because the risk is low. But if you could have tested and you chose not to, don't complain if you lose—but more important, don't get cocky if you win.

No Fear

Never start a business or an expansion when you're driven by fear.

In the recent economic downturn, we've seen people lose their jobs and start businesses because they couldn't find another job. That in itself is wonderful, and I believe that is what will drive the economic recovery.

Unfortunately, some of these would-be entrepreneurs are scared to death of being in business for themselves. They're starting their companies because they need a job and can't find one, and they're very much afraid that their businesses won't work. They're being driven by emotions, primarily fear, and it's very difficult to do what you have to do to build a successful business when you're afraid. Fear is a paralyzing, devastating emotion that has no place in business.

Don't confuse fear with commonsense best- and worst-case planning. In fact, going through the exercise of looking at worst-case scenarios and how you'll deal with them will help you overcome your feelings of fear.

Another great way to conquer fear is with industry knowledge. You'll be at a disadvantage if you don't have a tremendous amount of industry knowledge. Yes, it takes time to gain the necessary level of understanding of your particular business arena, but there are things you can do to speed up the process and gain the confidence you need.

When I bought my asphalt paving business, the main thing I knew about asphalt was that it burned my feet when I walked barefoot on the road as a kid. I had worked on a paving crew for about six weeks one summer when I was a teenager, but I was too young to operate the equipment, and I didn't really learn much about the technical process. But I wanted to buy a business. When I was reading the "businesses for sale" ads, this one caught my eye for a number of reasons. First was the ever so small bit of knowledge I had about the business. Second was the fact that I hated being cooped up in an office all day, and this was a type of business that would allow me to be outside. Third, and this one is really important, is that the owner said in the ad that he was willing to remain with the business for a year.

So there I was, knowing very little about asphalt, and buying an asphalt paving business. Some people might have been afraid to do that, but I wasn't. Having the previous owner stay on board with me for a year, to teach me the ropes and introduce me to the players, was key to getting over the disadvantages of my lack of industry knowledge. Yes, I had to pay him for that, but it was worth it. He was selling the company because he wanted to retire, so I paid him $2,000 a month for 12 months to teach me about the operation and the industry. This was above the amount that I paid for the company. His knowledge was so extensive that it saved me at least $200,000 in mistakes and wasted effort, because I would have done things very differently had I not known what the customs were—and I would have failed.

The first thing he did was take me on a job and show me how to run a paving machine and a motor grader. As the owner of the company, I wasn't going to spend my time operating heavy equipment—besides, I didn't want to do physical labor—but I needed to know how the equipment worked and the purpose of each

The Power of Words

Sticks and stones may break my bones, but words can never hurt me.

You probably learned this rhyme as a child and maybe chanted it to a playmate who was teasing you. It would be nice if it were true, but it's not. Words can hurt. They're powerful. It's not just how other people talk to you, it's how you talk to them—and how you talk to yourself.

For example, I don't have problems. Problems are negative, they're anchors that can drag you down, they're something the competition has to deal with. I may have challenges. I know I have opportunities. But I don't have problems. And you shouldn't, either. This is basic, but it can't be overemphasized.

People who hear you speak will respond subconsciously to the underlying message sent by your choice of words. That's why the best sales training courses spend so much time on this subject. This isn't just a bit of smoke-blowing that insists that all you have to do is say everything is great, and it will be. No amount of talking is going to accomplish anything unless you also have the right information and action to go along with it. But language is an important tool in your success arsenal, whether it's the words you use when you speak or when you think.

What you say to yourself and how you say it is more important than what you say to anyone else. After all, whom do you trust most in this world? Yourself. Whom are you going to believe, over and above anyone else? Yourself. So speak to yourself in language that will lift you up, give you confidence, guide you to the knowledge you need, and motivate you to achieve your goals.

machine. Next, he taught me how to find out about construction projects that I could bid on. That's an interesting process and one that a novice would find challenging. And if he hadn't explained all the unwritten rules to me, I would have wasted a tremendous amount of time bidding on projects I would never have gotten. Then he introduced me to the players in my market: the architects, the engineers, the contractors, the other paving companies, the construction companies, the material suppliers—everybody I needed to know to operate the company.

My point is: I had no fear of the asphalt paving business, even though I didn't know anything about it when I bought the company. I knew I was smart enough to run any business. I had the education, I could speak the language of business, and I knew I could learn whatever else I needed to know. So I went into that business with no fear—respect, certainly, but not fear.

If a business scares you, you're not going to be able to completely invest in it. You're not going to be able to take the financial and emotional risks; you're not going to give it all your energy and effort. You'll hold back and try to stay in a safe place—and it won't work. So if a business scares you, stay away from it unless and until you can figure out what you need to do to conquer your fear.

How Do You Track a Moving Target?

Being in business is like being on a perpetual hunt for multiple targets. The targets you have to keep your eye on are your market and your operating environment, and they'll never stand still. They'll always be on the move. At the very least, you have to keep up with them—and at the most, stay ahead of them. In fact, I spend about 90 percent of my time trying to figure out where our business is going to be next year and even five years from now and what we need to do in terms of marketing and operations to respond. CEOs that have good people working for them spend most of their time predicting where the market is going, what the economy is going to do, and how those things affect the company—and I have good people on my team.

JK Harris & Company was extremely successful during its first five years, but that was almost by accident because I wasn't looking at the future as I should have been. Had I been anticipating the future, I would have seen so many things—red flags and opportunities—that were staring me in the face, but I didn't notice them and I didn't deal with them. I don't know that paying attention to the future would have made a significant difference in our first five years, but I absolutely know that the impact on our second five years would have been substantial.

For example, my company became the target of an investigation by the IRS in 2000. That led to investigations by a number of state attorneys general, and those investigations led to some class action lawsuits against us. That blindsided me. I didn't see it coming, and I should have. I wasn't involved in politics, I wasn't proactive, I wasn't playing the right games. My business was growing, we were helping a lot of people who were in trouble and didn't know what to do, we were creating jobs and having a positive impact on the economies of hundreds of communities across the country—I thought all I needed to be doing was more of the same.

I was wrong.

I'll tell you more about these investigations and their impact on our organization throughout this book, but the lesson for right now is this: If I had been paying attention to the political environment and responding appropriately, I might have been able to prevent the investigations altogether, and if I hadn't been able to prevent them, I certainly would have been able to minimize them. But the target, which was our operating environment, moved—and I didn't notice.

It's easy to get so caught up in the day-to-day activities of running your business that you don't look any further into the future than the next fire you have to put out. But if you do that, you're risking your company's future.

For the first six months JK Harris & Company was in business, I did my testing and proved my business model. For the next four and a half years, I focused on implementing that business model, carrying out my plan. I had my hands full, and I didn't do a lot of planning beyond that. We had to open 400 sales offices, hire 80-something sales consultants, and hire enough tax and administrative people to handle the work as it came in. In five years, we went from 1 employee to about 400, plus 400 sales offices, with annual revenue of $38 million. The company's cumulative profits were $6 million. Any way you look at it, that's a successful business.

Those first five years were not without challenges. We survived the investigation by the IRS and all the related fallout from that—including negative publicity and a lender that canceled our line of credit. And we still grew at our planned pace and were profitable. I had no idea how different things would be in another five years.

At the end of the second five years, we were sitting on about $25 million in cumulative losses. Now, how do you go from a $6 million net worth to $25 million in cumulative losses in five years?

By losing sight of your targets.

We thought we were doing everything right. The numbers were beautiful. We were projecting *making* $25 million or more in that second five years, not *losing* that much. We were on top of the world—and we might have stayed there if I had been looking forward. But things we hadn't anticipated started happening. Yes, I know there are always going to be surprises in life and in business, but you can minimize those surprises by paying attention, being proactive, and tracking all your targets.

> "The measure of success is not whether you have a tough problem to deal with, but whether it is the same problem you had last year."
> —John Foster Dulles

So how do you track a moving target? With a combination of intelligence and smart guesswork.

Start with Where You Are

Take a high-definition snapshot of your business today. You need to see it clearly. Look at your industry. Who are the players and where are they—and you—in the big picture? Then look at your company. Study all the numbers, including the financials and the various statistics that measure growth, decline, and potential. Evaluate your people. Are they getting the job done? Do you have the talent you need? If you don't, is that talent available and what will it cost? Consider your location, your facility, your customers, your suppliers, what political issues are affecting you.

This is the time to be brutally honest—even if it hurts. If you don't know an answer, take the time to find out. Look at every asset and flaw. Whether you've been in business for years or are just getting started, you have to know where you are before you can identify and track your targets.

Where Do You Want to Be?

Create a vision of what you want your business to look like in 10 or 20 years.

I know some people will argue that we don't know what the world is going to look like in six months, so how can we create a 10- to 20-year vision for our companies?

The answer to that is simple: You have to do it. Without a vision, you won't get anywhere.

When I designed the model for JK Harris & Company, I had a very clear picture of what I wanted the company to look like in a year, 5 years, and 10 years. Today, the company is very close to what I envisioned back then. Yes, there were some detours along the way, as well as plenty of opportunities and obstacles that I didn't anticipate, but having the vision and staying committed to it kept us on track.

As you develop a vision for your company, it's safe to say that the only thing you can be absolutely certain of is that whatever you're doing today won't be sufficient in the future. Whatever kept your customers happy yesterday and even today won't make them happy tomorrow. Whatever marketing strategies worked last year will likely need adjusting for next year.

For example, in the beginning at JK Harris & Company, when it came to our customer relationships, we focused primarily on getting the work done and not so much on the emotional aspects of the situation for our customers. That worked then, because our customers had no real alternative for getting their tax debt problem solved. We pioneered the tax resolution industry. We were not only the largest, but our fees were set at a point that made us affordable to people who couldn't afford what a CPA or tax attorney would charge. At that time, the only other truly viable option for taxpayers in that category was to try to handle it themselves—and for most of our clients, that really wasn't an option. Today, those taxpayers have plenty of alternatives—and if you watch television even a small amount, you probably know who they are. We have had to change our operations because of that. Here's another example: Our early marketing strategies focused entirely on newspaper ads, which worked very well. But if we hadn't changed to add broadcast and internet ads to the mix, we'd probably be out of business by now.

And yet, I'll repeat: JK Harris & Company is today very close to what I originally envisioned in size, scope, and volume. It was because I had that vision that I was able to guide the company to this point. And it's because I still have a vision that we'll continue to grow and thrive. In fact, I have extended my vision for the company out another ten years, so I know what the company will look like then.

Create a Plan in Line with Your Vision

Once you know where you are today and what you want to be in the future, you can create a plan to make it happen. There are hundreds of books and programs out there that will guide you in the planning process—this book isn't about how to write a business plan. I will, however, highlight a few key points:

- *Your plan must be realistic.* Certainly it can be ambitious and optimistic, but it must also be fundamentally doable. If you can't create a realistic plan, you need to revisit your vision.
- *Put greater detail in your near-term plan than in your long-range plan.* The closer you are to implementation, the more the

Only Room for One Lead Dog

A good general rule is that a company can only have one leading entrepreneur. You certainly need executives, managers, and rank-and-file workers who think entrepreneurially, but you need one person who sets the direction and the tone of the business. I know I'm that person at JK Harris & Company (and not just because my name is on the company).

Ed Oates, who is one of the two software developers who founded Oracle with Larry Ellison, made this observation about Ellison: "Larry was the prime mover behind this thing. There was no question about the fact that Larry was pushing this idea a lot harder than either Bob or I would have pushed it. He had more chutzpah than the two of us combined. One and half times as much. So he got the chutzpah bonus. Bob and I both recognized that we were going to build the software, but this organization was going to be a success because of Larry's chutzpah."

The people who joined JK Harris in the first five years who are still with us and have helped build the company and have grown with the company did so because of my passion and vision for the future. I don't say this because of ego or an inflated sense of self-importance—it's the truth. We all know what our roles are, and because we do, we are able to play them to the max.

details matter. Getting too detailed about how you will do things that won't happen for a year or more is a waste of time.

· *Refer to the plan regularly.* Use the plan as a measuring tool to evaluate your progress. Take it out and look at it; don't count on what's in your head. Check your performance against your plan at least quarterly, maybe even monthly. Then once a year, update the plan and add the necessary detail.

· *Keep it flexible.* Certainly you need to respect your plan, but don't write it in concrete. Make changes when you have to.

In his book *Million Dollar Habits*, Brian Tracy writes, "An entrepreneur is like a guerilla fighter in the world of capitalism. . . . Perhaps the two most important habits you can develop in entrepreneurial thinking are those of speed and flexibility." Having a well-thought-out plan that's consistent with a clear vision will allow you to develop and apply the speed and flexibility you need to survive and prosper.

Do You Know if You're an Entrepreneur?

As important as it is to know what you don't know, there are some things you absolutely must know before you go into business. One critical thing is to know what your role will be. Not everyone is cut out to start and grow a business—and businesses need strong employees, good team players, people who like working at various levels in a company. Some of the best employees in the world, from entry level to senior executive, work at JK Harris & Company. They've been with me a long time and they're committed to the company. Every business owner needs a team of this quality. But first and foremost the business owner needs to be an entrepreneur.

I am an entrepreneur. I have known that from an early age. In fact, I knew it intuitively long before I was able to articulate it. I had been given the opportunity to be a leader while I was in military school, and I knew then that I would be a leader for the rest of my life—even if I didn't know exactly what I would lead. Once you get leadership in your blood, you can't get it out.

Of course, there's more to being an entrepreneur than just leadership. Though I knew at Carlisle that I wanted to lead, I also knew I didn't want to go into the military. Working for a big corporation, even as an executive in a leadership position, didn't have a strong appeal, either. I was willing to take risks, I wanted to be in control as much as possible, and I wanted to create something.

It was during my six months working at Connecticut General that it all crystallized for me: I would be an entrepreneur; I would own companies that would create jobs and provide goods and services the market would buy. Remember, Connecticut General sold life insurance to fund business buy-sell agreements. The policies were $1 million and up, and the target market was entrepreneurs—people who had built strong, profitable businesses and wanted to protect them. So in the process of working with the Connecticut General sales reps, I met a number of very successful entrepreneurs. None of them had ever had anything handed to them; they had all worked hard to achieve what they had. The majority of them started out in sales before going into business for themselves. They had built companies that were worth a lot of money, but they weren't really in it for the money. They were doing something they loved. They had become wealthy in the process, but some of them had also gone bankrupt more than once and been forced to rebuild. One of the gentlemen I met was in his 80s with a

> "I have always found that my view of success has been iconoclastic:
> success to me is not about money or status or fame, it's about finding a livelihood that brings me joy and self-sufficiency and a sense of contributing to the world."
> —Anita Roddick

personal financial worth that exceeded $100 million, yet he had been bankrupt three times in his life. These people didn't mind taking risks, but they were calculated risks. These were not reckless, careless people; they were thoughtful and deliberate, but they didn't waste time, energy, or resources. They knew who they were, they recognized what they didn't know, and they surrounded themselves with people who knew what they didn't—and that sounds a lot easier than it actually is.

What appealed to me about these entrepreneurs, and what I wanted for myself, was to build things, to create opportunities for people through jobs, to provide goods and services to meet a need in the market that wasn't being met at a price people could afford, and to make enough money to support my family, live comfortably, and give to the charities I believe in.

Operating at the Speed of Business

If I had to describe today's business environment in one word, it would be *fast*. It does no good to wax nostalgic for the "good old days" when things moved at a slower pace and you had plenty of time to make decisions and get things done—and it also does no good to debate just how good those days really were. The fact is, things have changed. And if you're going to be in business, you need to be able to operate at the speed of business. You need to know how to get to your flashpoint, and get there fast. The best way to do that is to be honest with yourself about what you don't know, figure out a way to either learn it or have ready access to someone who knows it, and be willing to take action when you don't have quite all the answers.

──────── **KEY LESSONS** ────────

✳ *Today's business environment is fast-paced, challenging, and unforgiving.* It requires flexibility, strong survival instincts, and a desire to build a company that meets a need in the market and creates jobs.

* *Success is a direct result of preparation and the right action.* You can't predict or control what's going to happen, but you can prepare and be ready to respond in a way that makes you a winner.

* *Choose to operate ethically and with integrity*—you'll sleep better at night, and that's worth more than any amount of money.

* *Business is driven by sales, and every business owner and manager can benefit from a basic understanding of sales techniques.* This will help you when you're small and can't afford to hire salespeople, as well as later, when you're building a strong sales team. Having strong sales skills will be a tremendous benefit in every other business and personal relationship as well.

* *Accept that you don't know everything, and commit to lifelong learning.* Read, study, listen, talk with people who know more than you do. Join professional associations and attend seminars. And don't be cheap about this. Certainly you want value for your education investment, but be willing to pay a reasonable price for worthwhile information.

* *Never roll out a marketing campaign or other business program without first testing it.* This allows you to fail small and succeed big. Money invested in testing is never lost, even when the test shows that the idea won't work.

* *Never start or buy a business when you're afraid.* If your motivation is being driven by fear, or if you're afraid the business won't work, you need to take a step back and deal with your emotions before you take your entrepreneurial leap. A realistic awareness of what might go wrong and a contingency plan to deal with such situations is not fear—it's smart. Fear is debilitating and can inhibit you from taking action and cause you

to make bad decisions. The good news is that fear can be conquered with knowledge.

* *Language is powerful.* Know what your words are really saying to yourself and others.

* *Business is full of moving targets, and you have to be able to track and hit them all.* Identify and set your sights on all your company's targets—not just your customers, but your competitors, suppliers, community, political environment, regulators, and so on.

* *Vision is critical.* Know where your business is today, where you want it to be in 10 or 20 years, and develop a plan that will get you there. Your plan will have to be flexible, but your vision should be consistent. Without a vision, you can't plan; without a plan, you will only wander around aimlessly until you fail.

* *Always know what your role is.* As an entrepreneur, you're the leader. Get out in front and stay there.

* *Get comfortable with the pace.* In today's business world, high-speed is the norm. Get used to it, or you'll get left behind.

Identify Every Player on the Field

Choose a niche, and know your market.

Whether or not you've actually followed it, that's excellent business advice, and you've probably heard it before. But there's more to it than those simple words might indicate.

There is, of course, absolutely no substitute for knowing your market—and no excuse for not knowing it. If you don't know who your customers are, how can you possibly develop marketing messages they'll respond to and create products and services they'll buy?

You also have to know every player in your industry. By every player, I mean your competitors, of course. In addition, you need to know the raw material and equipment suppliers, the manufacturers, the information and service resources, the regulators, the media—literally anyone who might at any point have some impact on your company. If someone is playing in your sandbox, even if it's just a very small corner of it, you need to know who they are, exactly what they do, and how they can affect you. When you know that, you'll also know how you can leverage yourself from their positions.

Know the Position and Operation of Any Entity That Can Affect You

Identifying every player in your arena isn't as easy as it might sound—nor is being sure of their position. But if you don't do it, someone can sneak up behind you and inflict some serious damage. When I launched JK Harris & Company, I thought I had done my homework. I knew the market, who the clients were, and who the competition was. I had a plan to differentiate my company from everyone else in the business and to quickly take the position of the industry leader.

What I didn't even think about was how government bureaucrats would look at our operation. We understood the nature of our customer, but the bureaucrats didn't. We learned the hard way that government bureaucrats, including the IRS, attorneys general (AGs), and consumer protection agencies, are key players in our field. We should have gotten to know them and taken a look at our business through their eyes from very early on.

Even though I had been a licensed CPA for nearly two decades when I started JK Harris & Company, I'd had very little in the way of dealings with the IRS other than the tax-related business of the companies I'd either worked for or owned and, of course, my personal taxes. But I knew my business, I understood tax law, I was a good accountant, and I was operating ethically and according to all the IRS regulations. I also know that when the IRS gets a complaint, they have to check it out. One key thing I didn't know was exactly how their criminal investigation division operated. I also didn't know that I was going to find out.

With Guns Drawn, Screaming and Yelling

At 9:02 A.M. on July 26, 2000, about 40 federal agents came bursting through the doors of our offices, wearing bullet-proof vests, with guns drawn, screaming, "Everybody freeze! Put your phones down! No cell phones! Step away from your desks!" We had mothers crawling under their desks, afraid that some crazy people had invaded the office and they were going to be shot.

It turned out to be the beginning of an IRS criminal investigation that would last three years and cost the government (meaning the taxpayers) millions of dollars to find out that we were doing absolutely nothing wrong. Here's how it happened:

Only CPAs, certified tax lawyers, and enrolled agents can represent a taxpayer before the IRS, so of course, we have a lot of them on our staff. We had this lawyer working for us, a guy who had moved from Virginia to Charleston when we hired him, who just couldn't seem to understand how we operated. Now, the way we handle cases isn't complicated. The first thing we do is get the client in compliance, which means arranging for all their delinquent tax returns to be filed so we know exactly how much they owe in back taxes and what we're dealing with. Then we get on the phone with the IRS and negotiate a settlement. We work hard to reach the best deal we can for the client. When we hang up, that's it. It's done. But this particular lawyer didn't want to do things that way. He was turning every case into a major production. He wanted to write ten-page legal briefs for the client; it wasn't necessary, it only confused the clients, and, most important, it didn't impress the people at the IRS, who are the people we must negotiate with. They don't have time to read that kind of stuff; they want the documents they ask for, and that's it.

We tried to work with this employee, to get him to do things the way they should be done, but he just wasn't getting it. In those days, we almost never fired anybody, but we terminated this guy. He requested an exit interview with me, and in that meeting, he told me that it was going to cost him $100,000 to move back to Virginia and get his practice started again, and he wanted me to pay him $100,000.

I pointed out that his contract said he would be paid $3,000 if we terminated him before the end of his three-month probationary period, which was what we did. He was a lawyer, and he read and signed his contract. I was sorry we couldn't make it work, but we were going to follow the terms of the contract he agreed to. I said, "Why would we give you more than $3,000?"

He said, "Because you are going to pay $100,000—you are either going to pay your lawyers, or you're going to pay me. You might as well pay it to me because that way you won't have to deal with all the lawyers." I thought he was threatening to file a lawsuit for wrongful termination or something. When I asked him what he was talking about, he said, "All it takes is one little letter to the IRS Criminal Investigation Division."

We weren't doing anything wrong, so I dismissed his threat. I wasn't going to be blackmailed into paying him $100,000 I didn't owe him—and I would have made the same decision even if I had known what was going to happen. At the time, I figured the IRS wouldn't give any credence to whatever charges he might concoct or claims he might make. It didn't occur to me that they would believe him.

One Surprise after Another

I later found out that he claimed we were running a Ponzi scheme, that millions of dollars were flowing through our office and out to secret accounts, and that we didn't have the people on staff in Charleston necessary to do the tax representation work for our clients. I also discovered that the name we knew him by wasn't his real name and that he had been disbarred under his real name in another state. I never did find out how he got a license to practice law under his new name.

A couple of years prior to this, there was a firm in California started by some former IRS agents that was billing itself as a tax representation firm, but instead of advocating on behalf of their clients with the IRS, they were teaching their clients how to hide assets from the government. It was illegal, a total scam. The IRS shut them down, and people were rightfully prosecuted. Thanks to this disgruntled former employee, the IRS thought we were doing the same thing.

We cooperated fully with the investigation, even though some of the tactics of the government's agents were questionable. For example, investigators called our employees at home to try to interview them without counsel present. They contacted former employees, asking for details about our "illegal" practices—which we weren't doing, of course, so those former employees couldn't help the government. Investigators also sent letters to our clients, asking questions about our representation of them. The only people they could find who had anything negative to say about us—besides the terminated employee who sent the original letter—were two other former employees. One was fired when we discovered he had lied about the status of his license to practice before the IRS. We found out that he had been indicted for conspiracy to defraud the IRS out of $28,000 in taxes. I think he offered to back the terminated lawyer's accusations against us in an attempt to plea-bargain. The other was a former IRS auditor who worked for us briefly but had difficulty moving to "the other side of the table" and becoming an advocate for the taxpayer rather than the IRS. This man had also worked closely with the agent in charge of the investigation when they were both auditors.

What made me angry then and still does today is that before the raid the Treasury Department contacted one of our senior executives, who, like many of our employees, was a former IRS agent, and told him that they had received accusations that they felt needed to be investigated. That executive immediately came to me, and my response was to have him tell the investigators that we would open our doors to them. They were welcome to see and copy any records they wanted and to interview any individuals they wanted. We had nothing to hide. They thanked him and said they'd be getting back with him. They "got back" with us by having armed agents wearing bullet-proof vests burst through the doors in a scene that you would expect to see on a television crime drama.

Even though we were completely cooperative, the investigation cost us dearly. We immediately had to retain defense attorneys for myself and 10 other employees that had been identified as targets of the investigation. Just the retainers for those lawyers was more than $100,000. So the terminated employee who made the threat was right about having to pay the money and, in fact, underestimated what his claims would ultimately cost me, because there was more than just legal fees to deal with.

Coincidentally at the time, our bank in California had been taken over by the FDIC, and government employees were looking at our line of credit. When they saw that the IRS was investigating us, they decided they needed to reduce the bank's exposure. I went out to meet with them, and they told me they determined that the subpoena and search warrant were sufficient grounds to call us into default on our $3 million line of credit. They gave me 30 days to pay them $1 million and 90 days to pay the other $2 million.

> "The fishermen know that the sea is dangerous and the storm terrible, but they have never found these dangers sufficient reason for remaining ashore."
>
> —Vincent Van Gogh

I was able to find the money on a short-term basis to get them paid, and then I went looking for a new long-term lender. Fortunately, we had a beautiful balance sheet—we were a very small risk for any financial institution. Once we got through the initial days after the IRS raid and were still

Give Them a Reason to Pay You

Do for your customers what they could do for themselves, but do it better than they could, and make it worth their while to pay you for it. The fact is that people can negotiate their own tax resolution with the IRS, but they're probably going to get a better outcome with far fewer headaches if a professional does it for them. We had to explain this to the attorneys general who were investigating us because they just couldn't understand why people were willing to pay us to do what they could do for themselves. But the reality is that people do that all the time.

People could do the same identity protection services for themselves at no cost that LifeLock does for its clients, but for many people, it's worth it to pay the LifeLock fee and have someone else handle it. Think about personal services such as housecleaning, dog walking, lawn mowing, and more—people could do these things for themselves. It's the same with business services—payroll, administrative support, travel and meeting planning, marketing services, and so on. Companies could set up their own internal systems to handle these functions, but it often makes more sense to outsource them.

There's not one single service we provide our clients that they couldn't do for themselves. But in most cases, we can do it better and more efficiently, and that's why they're willing to pay us to do it for them.

operating, I was sure we'd be fine. I was right, but there were still some challenges heading our way that I didn't foresee.

Then Came the Attorneys General

In the tax resolution business, our clients have one major thing in common: they all owe money to the IRS and/or some other tax collecting agency. But even with that commonality, the reasons they're in this trouble vary widely. Most of them are procrastinators. A substantial number of them haven't filed tax returns in years. Some of them are small businesses that owe payroll taxes. But though they come to us in debt to the IRS, and often to other creditors as well, most of our customers are honest, decent people who made mistakes or who were victims of circumstances. Yes, some of them made a deliberate choice to not pay a legal debt to the government, and they're hoping we can help them out. And even though their own nature is to procrastinate, they all want *us* to provide them with a quick fix. But the service we provide is rarely simple—and never quick.

If you run a restaurant and someone doesn't like a meal, you can simply apologize and replace the food at no charge, and you've usually resolved a problem and sent the customer away happy. If you have a retail store and a customer buys merchandise he isn't happy with, you can take it back and issue a refund. If you're a consultant and a client isn't happy with your performance, you can negotiate the fee to a mutually acceptable amount. My point is, in most businesses, you have total autonomy in deciding what to do and when to do it when it comes to dealing with unhappy customers and resolving problems, regardless of who is truly at fault and whether or not the customer's complaint has merit.

> *"Be a sponge. Spend as much time as possible with people who truly know their craft, and be a great listener. That is how you learn."*
> —Jerry Colangelo

Not so in the tax resolution business. We are bound by IRS rules and regulations. We do our absolute best to work out an arrangement with the IRS that our clients can accept that will bring them into compliance with their tax obligations. This is a process that takes time and requires certain actions from the client, such as providing us with information and documentation in a timely manner. The vast majority of our clients understand this, but there are some who want more from us than we can legally do, and some who expect the system to work faster than it actually does.

So we thought that, considering the nature of our business and our customer, a complaint rate of 5 percent meant we were doing a decent job. If we had 10,000 customers—people who owed back taxes and hadn't been filing tax returns—and 500 of them were not happy with the results we achieved, we were doing very well.

A Matter of Perception

Well, the bureaucrats at the various state consumer affairs agencies and attorneys general offices disagreed. We were in year seven of operation when this caught up with us. Some people argue that a regulatory agency complaint rate of 5 percent is more like a true complaint rate of as much as 35 percent, because 90 percent of the people who aren't happy won't bother to go through the process of filing a complaint with a state agency; they'll just forget about it. I don't know if that's true. I do know that attorneys general from 18 states banded together and came after us because of a complaint rate we thought was pretty good.

We're headquartered in South Carolina, and when all this started happening, our state AG joined the group of 18 AGs that were targeting us. After all, we were a South Carolina company and if we were committing fraud in his state, he wanted to be a part of the enforcement action. He was the only AG in the group that took the time to come to our office. He drove from Columbia to Charleston and spent several hours talking to our people. He didn't spend any time with me—I met him in the hallway and shook his hand but otherwise didn't say anything to him. He talked to our people who were actually doing the work, who dealt with the clients every day.

Then he left, went back to his office in Columbia, and wrote a blistering letter to the other AGs, accusing them of ganging up on a perfectly legitimate business that was trying to help people. He not only sent the letter to those AGs, but he released the letter to the media and substantial portions of it were published in the local newspapers. We never dreamed an AG would defend a business like that.

This situation gave me a valuable lesson in politics. The 18 AGs who were coming after us were Democrats; the South Carolina AG who defended us was a Republican. It doesn't matter which side of the political spectrum you're on, you have to understand how the political parties operate and interact. The 18 Democrat AGs were so angry with the single Republican AG for what they saw as a publicity stunt that I thought they were going to try to get an injunction to stop us from doing business in their states just to prove their position.

In the end, all the AG investigations resulted in no charges, just administrative actions. They didn't feel that we were doing anything illegal, but they wanted us to change some of our operations and marketing strategies. Some of the changes we made were no big deal; some of them actually made a positive impact on our organization.

We did have to defend our pricing to them, which was an interesting aspect to the whole process. The fees we charge make us one of the lowest-price tax resolution firms in the country. The average fee most of our competitors charge is $2,000 to $3,000 higher for essentially the same service. We operate on a high-volume, low-margin model; other tax resolution firms are low-volume, high-margin. But the AGs thought we were ripping people off for charging them $2,000 to do something they could do themselves. I tried to tell them that before I got into this business, it was costing individuals anywhere from $5,000 to $10,000 to get done what we were doing for $2,000. What's more, those individuals were filing just as many, if not more, complaints against the CPAs and tax attorneys they were using as we were having filed against us, but the AGs never heard about those complaints. The reason the AGs never got those complaints is that they weren't filed with the government; they were filed with a state's Bar Association (for an attorney) or the state's Board of Accountancy (for CPAs). And even if those complaints had made it to an AG, it's likely that they wouldn't have done much about it, because they were scattered among many small practitioners, not concentrated with one large one.

But a key lesson learned here was that we should have been proactive in realizing how regulatory and consumer protection agencies might view our numbers and helped them understand our business before the complaints escalated into investigations. Today, we contact the AG in every state in which we operate at least once a year. We ask if they've received any complaints or questions about us and, if they have, what we can do to help resolve the situation. We tell them that our goal is providing fair and honest service to our clients and that we want to address any issues that may arise before they escalate into major problems. These efforts have made our relationships with the various AGs far less adversarial than they have been in the past.

Something else I learned through this process is that in politics, even when you think you're getting some positive assistance from a politician, it can bite you. We thought we were getting help from the South Carolina AG who defended us, but it actually made things worse with the other AGs to have one of their own question their actions that strongly. Their demands doubled after that.

> "We act as though comfort and luxury were the chief requirements of life, when all that we need to make us happy is something to be enthusiastic about."
> —Albert Einstein

While explaining Strategy 1, I told you that at the end of our first five years, we had $6 million in accumulated profits, but by the end of the second five years we had cumulative losses of $25 million. The vast majority of that was in legal fees and settlements related to defending our company against the AG investigations and the vulture lawyers known commonly as class action plaintiffs' attorneys. What's more, we have no way of knowing how much business we lost because of the negative publicity.

Looking back, had I understood how AGs operate, I could have played the political game their way from day one, and things would have been very different.

The Long List of Players

The critical players I missed were obviously regulators, but there are plenty of others that could hurt you if you aren't paying attention to them. For example, you need to know who your suppliers and potential suppliers are—and you need to know your competitors' suppliers as well. If one of your competitors' suppliers went out of business or drastically dropped or raised prices, how would that impact your operation? Would your suppliers see an influx of business that might make it difficult for them to meet your needs?

Speaking of competitors, you also need to be aware of companies that aren't currently direct competitors but that might move into that position at some point. For example, is there a company serving a different geographical market that might move into your area? Or a company with a related product that might expand its product line to duplicate what you do? You don't have to spend as much time researching and monitoring these businesses as you do with existing competition, but you need to know who they are and have them in your line of sight in case you need to react to something they do.

Consider the transportation companies you depend on, whether it's to move freight or people or both. Are they financially healthy? Reliable? How would it affect you if one merged with another company?

Are any labor unions on your playing field? Many Southern states have what's known as right-to-work laws, which essentially means that labor union membership can't be a condition of employment. But just because you're in a right-to-work state doesn't mean you can ignore labor unions. What if a labor union representing the employees of one of your major customers or suppliers goes on strike? How will that affect your business? By the way, if your company isn't unionized and you want to keep it that way, the easiest way to do it is to treat your employees so well that they see union dues as a needless expense. Any union organizer will tell you that they can't get a toehold into companies that treat their employees well.

Take a look at the long-range development plans for the areas in which you operate and consider what that might mean to you. Every city or county is covered by a comprehensive master plan that, among other things, describes future land-use plans based on the anticipated growth of the area. If the zoning of the land you occupy or land near you changes, what will that mean to you? Or if a street is going to be widened, a new highway put in, or access to your facility changed? The plan is a virtual player on your field, and the people who control the plan are real players—get to know all of them.

As you study the other players, also think about everything that could affect them: man-made and natural disasters, labor disputes, regulatory issues, material availability, energy prices, and more. Add some players to your field that will serve as backups to your support team if you need them.

Sometimes the Competition Doesn't Compete

Most business owners consider their competition to be other companies that provide essentially the same or similar products and services that they do. For example, in our industry, we compete against other tax representation firms, as well as CPAs and lawyers that offer tax resolution services. It's traditional competition, based on service, price, and selling skills. I never dreamed that I would also have to compete against marketing firms. And if your business uses direct response advertising, you're probably competing against marketing firms, too. I don't know the exact numbers, but I wouldn't be surprised to learn that up to half of the direct response commercials you see on TV today are placed by marketing firms, not companies actually in the business.

These marketing firms are basically lead generators. They're typically small operations, often no more than one or two people working from their homes. They set up websites and contract with call centers, then they buy television time at bulk rates, create generic ads (which either don't give a company name or use a general name that's not an actual entity) for a particular service, then run their ads directing consumers to either call or go online. The call center or website gathers information from the prospective customer, and the marketing firm sells the leads it gets from those ads to the actual service providers. And, of course, in addition to their websites, the marketing firms also advertise prolifically on the internet so when consumers are searching for a provider or even just for more information about their problem, they're often directed to a website sponsored by a marketing firm.

> "A successful person is one who can lay a firm foundation with the bricks that others throw at him."
>
> —David Brink

This creates challenges for service providers in three primary ways. One is that these lead generators are buying up all the available television time. We've actually been unable to buy all the air time we want because the marketing companies have purchased so much of it. And when our advertising drops, we see a corresponding drop in sales and revenue. Second is that the lead generators often sell the leads multiple times, so you and your competitors might be paying for the same leads and contacting the same prospective customers. Third, they're creating confusion in the minds of the consumers. The generic ads and websites are designed to look as though they're an actual service provider, so consumers don't understand what's going on when they respond to one company and then receive sales calls from several others.

There is absolutely nothing wrong with the basic concept of these lead generation firms—in fact, it's an excellent business model for someone whose passion is marketing and a great resource for a company that wants to supplement its own marketing

You Need Thick Skin

There's an old saying that pioneers take the arrows and settlers take the land. If you're going to be out front in a leadership position, if you're going to be a pioneer, then you better be prepared to take some arrows. You're going to be misunderstood, criticized, and insulted. When you do something good, people will say you could have done more. When you do something wrong, it will be magnified.

If you have a tremendous need to be liked, to have people say nice things about you, don't start a business. Just about any true entrepreneur can tell you that when you start a business, people are going to say things about you and your company that are ugly and untrue, and may even cause you to question yourself. If your sense of self-worth is dependent on what others think of you, you don't have a thick enough hide to be in business.

Don't worry about what others think of you. It doesn't matter.

efforts. Of course, as in any industry, some lead generation firms are more ethical than others. What's important is that you understand that you may have competition from entities that aren't in your business. Know who they are, how they work, and have a plan for how you'll deal with them.

When You Need a Lawyer

There will be times in business when you need a lawyer. In fact, there will probably be plenty of times when you need a lawyer—and you'll need more than one. Lawyers specialize. You don't want an employment attorney defending you against a product negligence lawsuit. Because we live in such a litigious society, if you're in business, chances are good that you'll eventually get sued for something. Know that it might happen, prepare for it, and then don't worry about it. And if you get sued, don't panic. You'll have plenty of time between receiving the notice and before you have to take action to notify your attorney and figure out the best response.

It's a good idea to know who the best lawyers in your area are. That's part of knowing all the players on the field. Consult with them. Pay them a retainer. That way, you've got them locked up on your team. Your adversaries can't retain them because it would be a conflict of interest for the attorneys.

When the time comes that you're facing litigation, I have one piece of advice when it comes to choosing your attorney: As the head of my company's legal department says, "Retain the biggest son-of-a-bitch you can find."

Get Your Advice from Successful Entrepreneurs

According to its website, the U.S. Small Business Administration (SBA) is an independent agency of the federal government that "helps Americans start, build and grow businesses."

I'm not so sure about that. Yes, you can go to the SBA and they will tell you how to start and run a business, how to get all the necessary licenses and permits, how to keep your records and pay your taxes, and so on. But they're going to tell you that you need all of your ducks in row, your business plan completed, checked and double-checked, and absolutely everything just right before you open your doors. So if you have enough cash to survive a year or so before you can start making money, that might work for you.

I've heard stories of the SBA telling people it can take a year to get a business started. It took me a couple of months of research and planning, and then only one day to get JK Harris & Company going. One Sunday, I ran a newspaper ad—and I had a business the next day. I had more than 40 calls from prospective clients from that first ad.

Planning is important, but don't spend so much time planning that you never get around to taking action. When you're getting started, don't worry too much about aiming, just shoot the gun and then look to see if you hit anything. Jump into the deep end of the pool and don't worry about whether or not you can swim—if you have to, you can let yourself sink to the bottom, then push off to reach the surface. Yes, you need to be prepared. But preparation won't get you anywhere if you fail to act.

Most important, get your advice from people who have done what you want to do. Don't take financial advice from poor people and don't take business advice from people who aren't entrepreneurs. Now, the exception to that, of course, is advice on legal, accounting, and tax issues—but your advisors in those areas should be professionals who understand and think like entrepreneurs. They should be telling you how you can accomplish your goals, not why you can't.

> *"Try not to become a man of success. Rather become a man of value."*
>
> —Albert Einstein

Connections Count, but Sometimes They Backfire

In 1999, I recruited a former senior IRS executive, thinking he would shield us from IRS attacks. His resume was impressive: more than 35 years with the IRS, where he held a number of senior positions, along with being a respected speaker and author on tax topics.

It didn't help at all. In fact, they still raided us even after interviewing him—and he told them that we were operating legally and ethically. I've since been told that former IRS employees tend to cross the line of legality faster than tax professionals who have not worked for the IRS—and the IRS knows it. When you think about it, it makes sense. An IRS agent who has changed sides and is now working on behalf of the taxpayer has a pretty good idea of how far to push the envelope, and sometimes they'll push beyond what's legal. Their intentions may be good, but the methods may be unacceptable. And the IRS knows to watch these people more closely than someone who doesn't know where the IRS draws the line on what it's willing to overlook. However, let me stress that this particular former senior IRS executive never crossed the legality line. He was committed to helping our clients and he used his extensive tax knowledge to do that, but he always operated within the limits of the law.

We survived the IRS investigation because we had done nothing wrong, but it has investigated, indicted, and convicted competitors who were all former IRS agents.

My point is this: Sometimes you put people on your team expecting a particular result because of their connections, and you'll get just the opposite. By all means, use connections—just think through all the potential consequences.

Keep in mind that all successful people will have experienced failure at one time or another—and probably multiple times.

Learn from their failures. If they made mistakes, figure out what they did wrong and don't repeat it. If it was just circumstances that couldn't be overcome, study what they did so you can make better decisions if you are ever faced with a similar situation.

Most successful entrepreneurs love to share what they know. Take advantage of that. Knowing how other winners have done things right and what they've done wrong has helped me immeasurably over the years.

Playing the Political Game

When you have read the newspapers or watched news programs on television, you've probably seen the terms *lobby* and *lobbyist* used in ways that make you think they're profanity. Not true. Lobbying is simply the practice of influencing decisions made by government—and if you're in business, you need to be paying attention to what the government is doing and communicating with your legislators if you know of an action they are considering that would either help or hurt your company. I learned this lesson the hard way.

I always hated politics and refused to play the political games. In the past, I wouldn't hire a lobbyist, and I wouldn't do any of the other things that smart business leaders do to protect themselves in the legislative arena. But that's a shortsighted attitude that hurt my company. If I had been more proactive, things might have been very different.

Here's what happened: By 2003, our business was doing great, we were projecting profits of $5 to $8 million a year, and I decided it was time to diversify. It's not unusual for people who are in debt to the IRS to also be in debt to other creditors, so it made sense to create a subsidiary that could negotiate credit card debt settlements. I was aware that four states had passed laws prohibiting for-profit companies from negotiating credit card debt for their residents. I didn't see that as a problem—there were still 46 other states that would allow for-profit companies to offer that service. Moreover, I knew the need was there, and I knew that many of the people who were coming to us were also going to the credit card negotiators, so we could make the process easier for them by offering the additional service. And I knew the business had the potential to be very profitable, so I created a company that provided consumer debt negotiation services.

We invested $6 million and it took three years for that company to start turning a profit. But once it became profitable, it was *very* profitable. When we turned the corner from break-even to profitable, we had three months of $350,000 in positive cash flow. We could have recouped our $6 million fairly quickly at that rate. But in our third month of profitability, South Carolina passed a law saying that only nonprofit companies could negotiate consumer debt for South Carolina residents, and we had 30 days to get out of the business.

We were offering a good service that people needed, and we were doing a very good job on behalf of our clients. But with the new law, we had a choice: We could shut down or we could become a nonprofit. I decided to shut it down.

It would have been so easy to keep that $350,000 a month in profits and probably even grow it. The lawyers had it figured out. They said I could leave the for-profit company in operation and set up a nonprofit that would contract with the clients and do the debt negotiations. Then the for-profit company would handle all the advertising for the nonprofit, and bill the nonprofit for those services at an extremely profitable rate.

I told the lawyers I wouldn't do it. It wasn't worth the $350,000 a month profit, or ten times that much, for that matter, to know that I was committing fraud, even if they had figured out a way I could do it legally. What they were suggesting may have followed the letter of the law, but it certainly violated the intent of the law. I have to live with myself. To set up a nonprofit entity just to disguise the fact that you're running a for-profit business is unethical at the least. Also, in my opinion, the nonprofit debt negotiators were mostly frauds, and I wasn't going to be a part of doing business that way. Let me be clear that I know there are true nonprofit credit counseling and debt negotiation agencies that actually help people, but I think there are probably more scam artists than legitimate operations calling themselves nonprofit debt settlement agencies doing exactly what the lawyers told me I could do.

The lawyers looked at me like I was an idiot when I said no—who knows what they really thought of me? I didn't care. I'd been wrongfully accused of being a fraud by the IRS and the AGs, and I wasn't about to do anything that would make any of those accusations true. So in February 2007, we shut the debt settlement company down.

If I had been paying attention to the political landscape and, yes, if I had been lobbying the South Carolina legislature, I might not have been able to change the outcome, but I would have at least seen the law coming. However, I wasn't, and I didn't. I understand that the legislators were trying to protect consumers with this law; I could have educated them as to why it wasn't going to really do what they wanted, how scammers were going to get around it, and how to construct legislation that would truly keep consumers from being ripped off. But I was busy, I wasn't paying attention, and I missed the opportunity. These were very important players on my field that I ignored, and it cost me millions of dollars.

When you're looking at your field, be sure you see everybody.

KEY LESSONS

✳ *Knowing your market means knowing every player in your industry— your customers, suppliers, competition, regulators, and any other entity that could have an impact on your business.* Get to know the people involved and build relationships with them.

🔆 *Even when you're doing everything right, you can become the target of an investigation, and the entire process can make your life hell and hurt your business while you're defending yourself.* Don't spend a lot of time worrying about this until and unless it happens, but be aware of the possibility and what it could mean to your operation if it does. The best response to any investigation is to cooperate, but don't do it alone—always have competent legal counsel guiding you.

🔆 *Your perception of your operation may not be shared by outsiders, especially regulators.* For example, you may think a certain ratio of customer complaints is acceptable, but a consumer protection agency may disagree and charge you with misconduct, forcing you to defend yourself, possibly pay fines, and make changes. Be proactive, and help any outsiders who may be able to affect your company to understand the realities of your business.

🔆 *Identify and establish relationships with attorneys whose practices focus on the various areas you're likely to need legal advice with before you need them.* Remember that like doctors, attorneys specialize—don't ask a family law attorney to review your employment policies. Have attorneys you know and are comfortable with, and who know you and understand your business, on your team before a emergency situation occurs.

🔆 *If you offer a product or service that your customers can provide for themselves, do it better and more efficiently than they can so that they'll be willing to pay you for it.*

🔆 *Don't worry about what other people think of you*—it doesn't matter.

🔆 *Take your advice from successful entrepreneurs and others who have done what you want to do.* Don't accept counsel from those who don't have a track record you respect and admire. Keep in mind that successful people will have experienced their share of failure; learn from that so you don't repeat their mistakes.

* *Use your connections whenever it's appropriate and would benefit your business.* However, be aware of the potential of unintended consequences. Sometimes the result won't be what you expected.

* *Be active in politics.* No matter how busy you are, take the time to pay attention to pending legislation and invest time and money into lobbying lawmakers who can pass or defeat laws that impact your business. Make sure legislators recognize you as an industry authority.

Put the Right People in the Right Positions

Can you imagine a baseball team putting its best catcher on the pitching mound? Or a football coach asking his best linebacker to play wide receiver? That would certainly be an excellent strategy for losing—and a lot of decision-makers would be unemployed. So why, then, would you put someone who loves being around people in a job that's mostly solitary number-crunching? Or someone who likes rules, tradition, and structure in a position that requires creative, out-of-the-box thinking?

In *Jack: Straight from the Gut*, Jack Welch writes, "Getting the right people in the right jobs is a lot more important than developing a strategy." In my opinion, Jack had it partially correct. I say that getting the right people in the right jobs *is* a strategy—and a critical one at that.

The most efficient and effective way to get the right people in the right positions is through whole person assessments. This allows you to take a systematic approach to gathering information about individuals that you can use to make hiring and career development decisions.

I am a big believer in the value of assessments in the workplace. Done properly, this type of evaluation is an extremely effective human resources management tool that's easy to use and, thanks to technological advances, is affordable enough so that even small companies have no reason not to do it.

We've all experienced—or at least heard—the horror stories of employees who aced the interview and were absolute nightmares on the job. Less dramatic but equally frustrating are the candidates that seemed great in the interview but delivered a mediocre performance—not poor enough to warrant termination but not as good as you expected. Pre-employment evaluations in the form of a whole person assessment can significantly reduce those hiring mistakes. In fact, a whole person assessment is recommended by the Department of Labor as the most effective way to assess candidate performance potential.

What's It Really All About?

People hear the term *personality assessment* and tend to think of behavior, but it's more than that. Done properly, it's actually not just a personality assessment but a whole person assessment, which includes behaviors, values, attitudes, and skills. All behavior will tell you is *how* someone is going to do something. It doesn't tell you if they *will* do it or *why* they would choose to, or even if they're able and can do it. You deal with the *can* by training, but you can't do anything about someone's *why* and *will* motivation. In a traditional interview, you may be able to glean some insights into a person's behavior, but you can't tell what motivates them. You might ask, but they can fool you.

People who are suspicious of assessments don't really understand them. Assessments don't trick people into revealing their secrets nor do they invade anyone's privacy. They are not, in and of themselves, predictors of success. They simply tell you about the individ

"Every day I get up and look through the Forbes list of the richest people in America. If I'm not there, I go to work."

—Robert Orben

ual—is he or she an introvert or an extrovert? Creative? Artistic? Logical? A visionary? A leader? Reserved? Perceptive? Structured or loose? Dependable? Secretive? Patient or impatient? Idealistic or realistic? Able to deal with conflict or prefers to avoid it? You can certainly ask questions in an interview that might reveal these things, but you're far more likely to get a more accurate picture of someone through a standardized, proven assessment tool. You'll know from the assessment whether or not prospective candidates are a fit for the job and your organization, and if they don't quite fit, it will tell you if they're coachable and if they can *ever* fit.

Assessments give you a method to hire the type of person you know can do well in your company. It doesn't matter how well they did or might do in another organization or in a different environment; you need people who are right for the positions you have available in your company. If you take the time to understand what makes your peak performers tick, you can use assessments to determine if someone's personality is within the statistical variation range of the people who have proven to be the most successful in that occupation and then drill down to see if they're likely to be successful in *your* business. The stats can be provided by the testing firm, or you can use your own team to put them together. For example, you can look at the characteristics of your top sales performers and use testing to match those personalities with any new people you bring on board. When we started doing this type of benchmarking, the increase in our sales was dramatic.

Finding the Right Assessment Tool

You have a wide range of options when it comes to assessment tools. They include traditional knowledge and ability tests, personality and interest inventories, and performance tests. They'll differ in purpose, what they're designed to measure, format, and the level of standardization, objectivity, and quantifiability. Like any tool, assessment instruments can be extremely helpful when used properly, but counterproductive when used inappropriately. Most of the time, inappropriate use occurs when you don't have a clear understanding of what you're measuring and why. You need to know the purpose of the assessment to select the best tool that will deliver the results you want.

I first learned about assessments when I went to work as the corporate controller for Wikoff Color Corporation in Fort Mill, South Carolina, after selling my asphalt paving company. At Wikoff, absolutely everyone took a personality assessment as part of the pre-employment screening process. The production jobs, such as blending the inks to get the exact color required, were best done by people with a specific set of personality traits. Experience had taught Fred Wikoff, the company's founder, that hiring people without those specific traits didn't work—either they got bored and quit or they didn't do a good job and got fired. Management positions required a different set of characteristics, as did sales and administrative jobs.

As part of my interviewing process, Phil Lambert, the man who hired me and was my boss the entire time I worked at Wikoff, shared the results of my assessment, and it was right on the money. He explained that I had the exact personality they wanted for the job of corporate controller. I was impressed with that—but the next thing he taught me impressed me even more.

The woman who prepared and maintained the payroll records reported to the corporate controller. She did a good job, but she had some quirks that weren't always easy to deal with. For example, she was very sensitive. If you looked at her wrong, she would start to cry. You couldn't raise your voice around her or she would assume she was being yelled at, even if all you were doing was asking her from across the room if she wanted a cup of coffee. But her sister was Fred Wikoff's wife, and he owned the company, which meant that her job was far more secure than mine would ever be. In fact, my boss made it very clear to me that if she ever went crying to Fred, complaining about me, I would be in trouble.

Like all employees, she had taken a personality assessment. Phil explained to me what I had to do to get along with her and get her to do what I needed. It wasn't difficult; it just required an awareness and understanding of how she related to others. I followed his advice, and it worked. Had I not known how to deal with her, I wouldn't have lasted more than a few weeks. Instead, I was with Wikoff for four and a half years and gained knowledge and experience that have been tremendously valuable to me in every venture since.

Not Good or Bad

Another important lesson Phil taught me was that an individual's characteristics aren't good or bad—they simply are. Before he hired me, he showed me the graph of my personality assessment. He said, "See this spike here? The first thing this is showing me is that you could have some serious problems with some of the people who work in our accounting department." I asked how a spike on a graph could show that, and he said, "That spike is telling me that you're extremely intelligent and that you don't suffer ignorance in others. You could easily be insulting and talk to people like they're stupid. You don't mean to, but because things are so simple to you and make so much sense to you, you don't understand why the person sitting with you can't figure it out."

He was right. In the paving business, I worked with a bunch of people who definitely weren't the sharpest knives in the drawer, and I didn't have a lot of patience with them. I would lose my temper and talk to them in a very patronizing, insulting way. In fact, I ran off quite a few people who worked on my paving crews because of the way I treated them. At Wikoff, the basic accounting jobs didn't require a high degree of intelligence and would actually be boring to someone with a bright, inquisitive mind. So they hired people who would be satisfied with doing repetitive work day in and day out. That type of person isn't always a quick learner. They're not necessarily stupid, although they may be slow to grasp new concepts and to make changes in the way things are done. But they're essential to getting the routine work done in any operation.

Once I understood that a lack of patience with people who don't learn as quickly as I do was a basic part of who I am, I was able to control my behavior and how I related to others. Of course, at first I went to the opposite extreme—instead of risking insulting someone by trying to explain something, I would simply do whatever it was myself. It took me some time to find the right balance of knowing when to explain and when to give up, and it's something I still have to work on. But having the understanding that this is part of my personality makes it easier.

> "Achievement seems to be connected with action. Successful men and women keep moving. They make mistakes, but they don't quit."
>
> —Conrad Hilton

So I learned that while this personality trait could manifest itself in a negative way, it wasn't in and of itself a negative thing. It's who I am. Phil also told me that people who have this personality trait often strike others as being arrogant know-it-alls, and you can't tell them anything. That really

A Word of Caution

The number of laws and guidelines governing employment practices has increased substantially over the last 40 or so years. Be sure the assessment instruments you use are fair and unbiased to all groups; that they've been demonstrated to be valid for the specific purpose for which they're being used; and that they're appropriate for the target population.

bothered me. This conversation took place before he offered me the job, and as we sat there and talked, I was certain that I was wasting my time and his. But then, after telling me what potential trouble I could be for him, Phil hired me. And in that process, he made it clear to me that I am who I am, and others are who they are, and I wasn't going to make it in that job with that company unless I understood that. It was a lesson that has served me well ever since.

After learning that, I became fascinated with assessments and began studying them. I found out that the personality assessment Wikoff used was only the tip of the iceberg—it was strong, but the real power of the process came through doing whole person assessments.

It's about Good Matchmaking

You want every person you hire to have the basic tools to succeed, and a critical part of that is being sure the individual's personality is a good match for the job. If you put someone in a position who has a personality that's the complete opposite of people who do well in that role, you're hurting them and your company.

You also want to make sure that every person you hire is a match for your company's culture. It's important to do an assessment that tells you whether or not someone has the personality and inclination to do a particular job, but you also have to take that process to the final step, which is to make sure the person will fit your company culture. The culture is the way things are done every day. Your positions must be benchmarked in your culture as well as the basic skills and abilities required by the job. Then you can hire people to fit your benchmarks. If you want successful people, you have to determine what works in your culture.

According to Wikipedia, a company's culture is the total sum of the values, customs, traditions, and meanings that make a company unique. Basically, it's the way things get done. A company's owner and senior managers play a significant role is setting the culture, but they can't totally dictate it. At least some of it will evolve on its own. And you need to be sure you—or the people making your hiring decisions—have a clear and honest picture of your culture. Your employees' value structures have to be supported, rewarded, and condoned in the culture. If they're not, people will show up, but they won't be engaged—they'll be focused on what's truly important to them, which may be somewhere else. You want people who are going to be compatible with your culture so that they can be committed to your company.

> "If you want to build a ship, don't drum up people together to collect wood and don't assign them tasks and work, but rather teach them to long for the sea."
> —Antoine de Saint-Exupery

Most people don't understand that their personalities make them suited for certain roles and organizations and unsuited for others. This means you can't depend on them to tell you in what positions they're likely to excel because they don't always know. If you put someone in a role where the probability of failure is high, you could do permanent emotional damage to them. I don't ever want to

Allow Room to Move

Micromanaging is the kiss of death to a growing business. Whether you're an owner, a senior executive, or a midlevel manager, you need to give your people room to work. Step out of the day-to-day operation. If it can't function without you, figure out why not, go back in and fix the problem, and then get out of things again. But if you're staying on top of every minute detail, you'll choke the life out of your company—and you won't be doing yourself any good, either.

be responsible for harming anyone just because they aren't a good fit with my company. And when people don't do a good job because they can't—because they're in the wrong position with the wrong organization—you're costing your company money and opportunity. It's absolutely not fair to your people and to your business to not do a whole person assessment on each of your employees.

Using Assessments to Benchmark

A basic business success strategy is duplication. Find something that works and duplicate it. That's exactly what franchising is all about: a company figures out a format that works and grows exponentially by duplication. Assessments allow you to duplicate your top performers by benchmarking their characteristics and then hiring other people who are like them.

Benchmarking in all aspects of your operation is important—in human resources, it's critical. It's essential to know exactly what works and what doesn't.

As logical as this concept sounds, less than 5 percent of American companies assess their employees and make hiring decisions based on established benchmarks. Yet this is such a simple and obvious thing to do: Look at the people who have done well in your operation and hire other people who are like them.

Small Companies Are No Exception

If you have even one employee, your company is big enough for personality assessments. I learned that the hard way when I opened my first accounting practice.

Though I am a CPA, I am not, by nature, a bean-counter. I don't like doing accounting work. I'm an entrepreneur. So when I started my accounting practice in 1996, I hired a young CPA, fresh out of school, to handle the actual accounting work for my clients. I focused on the marketing and sales. Once the clients were on board, I took her out to meet them and tried to get her to establish a relationship with them so I would be free to spend my time prospecting for new clients. I knew that was the only way I could grow the practice.

If One Is Good, More Are Better

Don't rely on a single test. Use a whole person approach to assessment. Remember, someone could have the perfect personality for a job but not have the necessary skills, or have the skills but not the personality, or have both the skills and personality but not be a fit for your culture. The components of a whole person assessment include

- achievement tests
- aptitude tests
- general ability tests
- interest inventories
- interviews

- personality inventories
- physical ability tests
- specific ability tests
- work samples/performance tests
- work values inventories

My fatal mistake was that I didn't check her personality. After working with her for a while, I realized she was an accountant's accountant—a true bean-counter, where I was a true entrepreneur. I was the first contact with new clients—most of whom were also entrepreneurs—so we bonded during the sales process. Then I would introduce them to my staff accountant and move on to finding more clients. That transition from me to her was horrible—absolutely horrible. She was a terrific behind-the-scenes person, but she just wasn't good with people. The clients got angry when she would show up instead of me. They actually said that they were paying me, not her; that they hired the firm with my name, which meant they wanted me doing their work, not someone else—especially not someone who wasn't an entrepreneur, who didn't think like they did, who just wanted to put the numbers in the right place on the page and have everything balance.

I should never have hired that individual for that position. I shouldn't have hired someone who was quiet, reserved, and withdrawn to deal with outgoing, exuberant entrepreneurs. She wasn't happy, and my clients weren't happy. I knew her, I knew my clients, and I should have known it wouldn't work. If I had been using the personality assessment tool the way I was taught at Wikoff, I never would have hired her.

The two lessons here are: 1) No company is too small to use assessments in hiring, and 2) it's part of human nature that we don't always do what we know to be the best thing for ourselves and our companies. When you know what the best thing is, do it— no excuses.

The Sales Team That Couldn't Sell

After JK Harris & Company had been in operation a couple of years and had about 40 salespeople on board, I realized that our sales were flat and the only way I was going to be able to increase revenue was to increase the fees we were charging. But I didn't feel the market could bear higher fees. Our business model was designed to target people who couldn't afford to pay more. Our fees were sufficient for us to make a profit, but we needed volume, which was why I really wanted to increase the number of sales we were making. Because I believe in continuing education, I brought in Greensboro, North Carolina–based The Brooks Group to provide sales training to our consultants. I was expecting them to immediately put on some seminars—after all, we were the customer and I had asked for sales training, so I was expecting to get what I asked for—but instead they insisted on doing an evaluation of our sales team using an assessment tool before they did any training at all.

Even though it wasn't what I was expecting, this made a lot of sense, especially considering what I had learned at Wikoff. In fact, I took the test along with all the salespeople. When Bill Brooks, founder of The Brooks Group, and Richard Dickerson sat down with me to give me the results of the assessment, they nailed me to a T. And I just laughed, because it was virtually the same assessment that I was given 25 years earlier when I went to work for Wikoff. I hadn't changed, and Bill told me that I wasn't going to change, either. This is who I am. I can learn skills to enhance my personality, but the basic, essential me is never going to change—and the same thing applies to everyone else. You are who you are.

> "Leaders are visionaries with a poorly developed sense of fear and no concept of the odds against them. They make the impossible happen."
> —Dr. Robert Jarvik

You can learn, you can adapt, but you can't change the essential you.

The good news of this process was that—thanks to my experience at Wikoff and the results Bill and Richard showed me—I knew that these tools were accurate and effective. The bad news was that the tools revealed that only about 25 percent of the people I had out there selling our services were qualified from a personality or natural inclination perspective to be salespeople. I didn't have a team of salespeople; I had a team of people who were primarily order-takers. They were good people, they understood our business, they cared about our clients, and they worked hard. But they weren't salespeople, and no amount of training was going to change their personalities. Before the sales training had even begun, I realized I was going to have to replace 30 of the 40 people I had in sales.

This was a gut-wrenching realization for me. I had been running the sales force for two years and had developed close friendships with many of our sales consultants. They had become like family to me, and I had to sit them down and tell them they needed to find a different profession. But as painful as it was, I did it—I'll tell you more about that when I tell you about Strategy 5—and today we have an absolutely outstanding team of sales professionals who are superb at matching the needs of our clients to the services we offer.

Beyond Hiring

As a hiring tool, assessments help you put people into jobs that suit their basic personality and abilities and to screen out people who wouldn't be a good fit for your jobs or culture. But assessments have a number of other uses. If you decide to implement pre-employment assessments, it's a good idea to go ahead and assess all of your existing employees as well. You'll gain a valuable tool to use when evaluating candidates for promotion. Another benefit is learning how to best deal with someone you'd like to keep but who's not doing well—a personality assessment can help you figure out how to manage that person better or to identify a different position that would be a better fit.

Another use for personality assessments is management. It's a very effective tool for teaching supervisors and team members how to understand what motivates each other. If you have a personality assessment on every member of a particular team, you can help the team leader understand how to best manage each person. By applying this tool to every member and position on your team, you'll build an unbeatable operation.

At JK Harris & Company, we try to promote from within, so most of our supervisors began working with us in the position they're now supervising. Most of them have at least some college and many hold degrees, but they tend to be young and often have no supervisory experience when we promote them. We have to train them, and part of their training is that they learn that not

Truth Be Told

Is it possible to trick a personality assessment? Sure. But you'll usually be able to determine fairly quickly if someone has tried to do that.

Our prospective employees take the assessment online. On rare occasions, an applicant will have someone else take the test for them, but we usually realize very soon after hiring—and sometimes even before—that the individual who actually answered the assessment questions isn't the individual we're working with.

Can someone skew the results by not being honest when answering the assessment questions? Yes, but that's usually apparent when the results are evaluated. The questions are structured in a way that provides what amounts to cross-checking, so if, for example, an introvert tries to make himself look like an extrovert, the assessment results are going to indicate that something isn't right.

During the initial screening process, we make it clear that the assessments are a tool that benefits both the company and the employees, and that honesty when completing them is critical.

everyone can be managed the same way. Then we follow that up with giving them the very specific tool of understanding the personalities of the people they'll be supervising.

Our executive vice president of sales and marketing knows the results of the personality assessment of each one of his regional managers. And each one of the regional managers knows the results of the personality assessment of their sales consultants. They all use this information to communicate more effectively with each other, to understand each other better, and help everyone on the team stay motivated, positive, and upbeat. We have sales consultants who need to be hounded if their numbers are off—and we have sales consultants who need to be nurtured if their numbers are off, because if they get hounded, they will tighten up and things will get worse.

Size Doesn't Matter

Personality assessments used to be so expensive that only big companies could afford to use them. In the "old days," it could cost as much as $300 to have an assessment done. Today, you can have an assessment done for as little as $25 per person—and that's a small investment to avoid a big hiring mistake.

The key to successfully using assessments is that the business owner and maybe even a few of the senior executives need to commit to going to school to learn how to interpret and use the test results. Some testing companies will also offer the evaluation for an additional charge, but it's worthwhile to learn how to do it yourself. Not only will it make you a better manager, but it will also make you a better human being.

> "There are people who make things happen,
> there are people who watch things happen,
> and there are people who wonder what happened.
> To be successful, you need to be a person who makes things happen."
>
> —Jim Lovell

Prepare for Some Pushback

Some people are very intimidated by the idea of taking an assessment test—and unfortunately, the assessments look like tests, with a list of questions and a selection of answers. The thought of taking a test drives some people into a panic over a fear of failing. You have to work hard to communicate with these folks that this isn't a pass-fail exam. Another reason people are intimidated is the concern that the assessment will reveal private things about them—it won't. Their secrets will be safe.

When we began giving the same personality assessment to our production team that we had used with our sales force, you would have thought from their reactions that we were threatening their lives. I assured everyone that no one was going to be terminated over the results of their assessments, that we had been using this tool with the sales force for years, and we felt this was a tool that could improve communication and performance across the board. We identified three common characteristics among our top production performers, and now we keep that in mind when we make hiring decisions. And yes, productivity is improving.

Dealing with Fear

Whether your candidate or employee obviously demonstrates such feelings, many people panic at the thought of taking a test as part of a pre-employment or career development assessment. You probably know people who are very intelligent but did poorly in school because they freeze during a test. Be sure that whoever is administering the test takes the time to explain why the test is being administered, how the results will be used, and that the results will be confidential. And if for any reason you suspect the results are not valid, consider retesting or using an alternative assessment.

When People Don't Fit

It's not always easy to correct a hiring mistake. For example, a person may not be doing a great job, but he may not be doing a bad enough job to justify termination. And then there's the situation

Give Them Room to Grow

Once you've got the right people in the right place, don't enclose them with restrictive boundaries. Give them the room they need to reach their full potential. That's what Dave Liniger did when he founded RE/MAX, one of the largest real estate networks in the world. In the beginning, Liniger thought his business was all about market share, but then something happened that made him realize it was about giving people the space and care to grow.

After Liniger's wife, Gail, had been seriously injured in a plane crash, he bought her a glass terrarium. Her recuperation took three years, during which she was in and out of the hospital, and Liniger took care of the terrarium. But he wasn't very good at caring for the small plants. When he told Gail he wanted to throw the unhealthy-looking terrarium out and buy her a new one, she wouldn't let him. She was, understandably, sentimentally attached to the gift he had given her right after the crash. So he decided to repot the plants instead.

Once free from the confines of their glass container, the plants from the terrarium began to grow. Today, those small plants Liniger wanted to throw away are almost ten feet tall and thriving in the couple's Denver home. That's what RE/MAX is all about, Liniger says: removing barriers and giving people the freedom to be something bigger.

Don't impose artificial boundaries on your people, and don't let them do it to themselves. Give them room to grow and let them wow you with what they can do.

flashpoint

that often happens in entrepreneurial companies where family members of either the owner or other employees have been hired when they're not really suited for the job, but you're either stuck with them because maybe they're a relative of the boss or a relative of a valuable employee, and you don't want to risk creating a problem with the employee you need by terminating the one you don't. This has happened to me more times than I can count over the years.

If you didn't do a personality assessment when you hired, it can still help you deal with a situation like this. When you get the results, sit down with the employee and just lay it on the line. Explain that the position needs someone with certain personality traits, and that individual's traits are not a match. Can that person do the job? Maybe. Will that person excel at the job? No. Then explain that you need people who will excel and talk about positions where that person is better suited. You'll probably find that the person is relieved because he hasn't been happy.

It may be that you don't have a position that's appropriate for someone with those personality traits. In that case, offer to help the person put together a plan that will get him in a position where he fits, even if it means allowing time during the workday for a job search.

And if it's a situation like I was in at Wikoff with the owner's sister-in-law where you're stuck with the person, use what you know about the individual's personality to make the best of difficult circumstances.

Work Force Stability

Work force stability is a key to any company's longevity. Turnover is not only expensive from the practical dollars and cents perspective—the cost of recruiting, hiring, and training—it also means that you lose a sense of the company's history. That "corporate memory" is important, and it takes workforce stability to develop it.

A stable work force also means that your people get to know each other and build strong relationships, and, in a positive upward spiral, those relationships contribute to the stability of your work force. People who have strong bonds with their co-workers are less inclined to see the grass as greener on the other side of the fence.

When you commit to putting the right people in the right positions, you have established the foundation for work force stability that will serve your company well.

Employees Are Customers, Too

It's understandable that your employees will be more relaxed and casual with one another than they are with customers, especially among peers who have worked together a long time. That's fine, but it's not a license to be rude and unresponsive to co-workers. Don't treat your employees any differently than you treat your customers, and don't let your employees treat each other differently than they treat customers. In fact, create a culture where your employees treat each other *like* customers: with respect, courtesy, and top-notch service.

The Customer-Focused Benefit

Our employees used to just come to work and do a job, go home, and collect their paycheck. Once we revised our mission statement to a customer-centered message that was easily understood and invested in communicating that message to everyone in the company, we've seen a tremendous increase in the pride and dedication of each person on the team. They understand not just *what* they're doing, but *why* they're doing it.

The JK Harris & Company mission statement is: "The JK Harris mission is to deliver financial and tax representation services with the highest levels of ethics, advocacy, and client satisfaction." There's absolutely no ambiguity in that statement; everyone knows that their first priority is to the customer, and we remind them by making the statement visible in multiple places around the office, including on their computer log-in screens.

They'll Stick Around When They're Appreciated

It's important to figure out what motivates people and provide that as an incentive. The challenge is that when you have a company, you have a lot of people with different motivations. You might have some people who are motivated by recognition and public praise and others who don't care about that but want the reward in their paycheck or in some other tangible form.

This doesn't mean that you shouldn't publicly recognize people who don't really care about that, because that public recognition will be noticed by the people who are motivated that way. That you recognize people in general will be a motivator for the people who crave recognition. That you express your appreciation in a variety of ways will be a motivator for people who are driven by needs other than recognition. Of course, your monetary rewards need to be based on objective, measurable criteria that apply to everyone. Make your other expressions of appreciation meaningful—for example, don't bother arranging for a dry-cleaning pick-up and delivery service if everyone dresses in jeans and T-shirts, but if you have a lot of employees with young children, discounts at kid-friendly places would probably be very much appreciated.

The bottom line is: Take care of your people, and they'll not only take care of your company, but they'll take it to the flashpoint.

--------- KEY LESSONS ---------

* *Be sure the people you hire are a good fit for their positions.* To do this takes more than simply reviewing their applications and

conducting a few interviews. Use a whole person assessment to hire the right people.

- *Keep your company's culture in mind as you hire.* Be sure people can not only do the job you need but that they'll be comfortable in your environment.

- *Understand how assessment tools work.* They're not measurements of good and bad; they just tell you what is. When you understand who a person is, you can make a decision about whether or not they're right for your company.

- *Assessment tools can help you in day-to-day management as well as in career development for your employees.*

- *Use assessment tools to identify benchmarks for hiring and promotions.* Take a look at your top performers, benchmark their characteristics, and hire more employees who are like them.

- *The cost of doing pre-employment and career development assessments isn't an expense, it's an investment.* It's also not something only big companies can afford to do; it's something smaller companies can't afford *not* to do.

- *Assessment tools are extremely reliable.* They have built-in verifiers, so you can tell if someone is trying to trick the process.

- *If you realize that you have people in positions for which they're not suited, even if they're doing an adequate job, replace them with people who are suited for the job. Do it with kindness and compassion, but do it.* Though it will likely be a painful process, it will be better in the long run for the employee as well as your company. If possible, transfer the employee to another position within your organization; if not, help them put together a plan to move on.

- *If you begin using assessment tools with existing employees, be prepared for some negative reactions.* Take the time to thoroughly communicate what the tools will and won't do and reassure people that the assessment won't be an invasion of their personal privacy.

✳ *Don't micromanage.* Hire good people, and get out of their way. Let them do their jobs.

✳ *Work force stability is essential to a company's longevity.* Hire the right people for the right positions, treat them well, recognize their achievements, and express your appreciation.

Know Your Market, and Market Constantly

K now your market. When I say this, I mean know *everything* you possibly can about your market—your customers, your influencers, your competitors. When you know your market, you can position yourself in it in the most advantageous way. This isn't rocket science. It's not cutting-edge advice. It's basic business.

There's absolutely no excuse for not knowing your market, and yet, it's amazing how many business owners and managers know very little about their market. When people come to me for advice about their businesses, it's often clear to me from the way they answer my questions that while they may completely understand their product, they're absolutely clueless about their market.

The process of studying your market may not be the most exciting part of being in business, but it's essential—especially when the economy is tight. Remember, it's easy to be successful when the economy is booming. You can have all kinds of business and not have any idea where it's coming from or why people are buying from you. But if you don't know your market and the economy either goes flat or takes a downturn, you're not going to know how to respond.

Go to the Experts

When it comes to marketing, the best advice I can offer is this: Don't reinvent the wheel. Find a marketing expert who knows your industry and your customer, and be willing to pay to learn what that expert knows.

When I decided to open my CPA practice, I didn't know anything about starting and marketing a professional service firm. The internet was just starting to get popular then, so I went online and found a marketing program designed specifically for CPAs. It was a direct response, direct mail marketing program from Mostad & Christensen, and it included some very powerful marketing letters. It was my first exposure to emotional direct response marketing, and I became fascinated with it. This company had clearly researched and tested their program, because the letters worked, and I was able to use them to establish the client base I needed in just a few months. I couldn't have done that by myself.

Later on, when I realized the potential of the tax representation business and decided to change the focus of my practice, the expert that I found was Jack McDonough, founder of U.S. Tax Marketing Corporation in Littleton, Colorado. Jack had sold his traditional CPA practice in 1992 after the IRS liberated its decades-old policy of not entertaining settlement offers where the delinquent taxpayer was offering to pay less than their full assessed tax liability. By the time I got into the business, Jack had five years of experience in marketing to this target client. He had put together a turnkey business and marketing plan that he was selling in a three-ring binder for $895. The paper and the notebook probably didn't cost $5, but the business knowledge he was selling has been worth millions to me.

There are plenty of similar products on the market that cover just about every possible endeavor. It seems to be a common trait among businesspeople that when we learn how to do something well, we want to share that knowledge. Even if you're already in an established business, take the time to get and read some of the startup guides out there for your type of business. You'll probably pick up at least a few new ideas from each one.

Using primarily the information in Jack's manual, I launched JK Harris & Company. Later on, after we were up and running, I consulted another expert: Britt Beemer, founder of America's Research Group, Ltd., a consumer behavior research and strategic marketing firm in Charleston, South Carolina. I wanted to confirm that everything I had learned from Jack McDonough's manual was still applicable. I also wanted to find out if the marketing messages we were using were still the best messages to get people to pick up the phone and call us.

Britt's team did a market research study for us that provided us with some very valuable information. A key result of the study was that we were finally able to determine the size of our market. Prior to that, we could only guess at the number of people who owed back taxes. The government doesn't release information on how many individuals and businesses are in debt to the IRS. Our first study showed that about 8 percent of households were in debt to the IRS; a follow-up study we did a few years later refined that number to 6 percent.

Another key piece of information we gleaned from the study was that the public perceived that a former IRS agent could get them a better deal on

"The opposite of a correct statement is a false statement. But the opposite of a profound truth may well be another profound truth."
—Niels Bohr

settling their tax debt than a CPA or tax lawyer. The reality is the opposite. The majority of ex-IRS agents are not good advocates for taxpayers; most of the time, they'll side with the IRS in any dispute or negotiation. They tend to think of delinquent taxpayers as deadbeats, and that's how they treat them. There are a few of them who are aggressive and will fight for their clients, but most are (pardon the expression) lay-downs when it comes to how they deal with their former employer.

We've always had former IRS agents on our team. We're selective about which ones we hire, because so many of them simply can't deliver the level of customer service we require. But even though we know that the best people to handle the tax resolution process are typically not ex-IRS agents, we also know that we aren't going to be able to change public perception, so we emphasize our former IRS agents in our marketing. Without the study, we wouldn't have realized what a strong marketing hook that is.

The study revealed that a lot of things we thought were true about our customers were actually not, and we modified our marketing accordingly. At the same time, we confirmed that the

Be Realistic

When it comes to assessing your market, you have to be honest with yourself. Don't convince yourself that a market for a particular product or service exists just because you want to provide that product or service. Just because you think people need something doesn't mean they want or will buy it. Don't assume that an existing market can support an additional provider. If new players enter the field, there may not be enough business to go around. And don't take for granted that the market that exists today will still be there tomorrow. Markets change—they grow and shrink, and sometimes they disappear.

original plan I bought from Jack McDonough was still on target. The study also gave us information that Jack's material couldn't, such as the search terms people with tax problems used, because Jack put his program together in the early '90s, back before virtually everybody was browsing the internet.

You can do some market research on your own and learn a good deal, but it really pays to hire an expert who has access to data and research skills you don't. If you don't consult a market research expert, you may as well just go outside with a wad of hundred-dollar bills, start throwing them up in the air, and hope they'll stick to a few people who might want to become your customers

What Business Are You In?

Do you know what business you're actually in? We tend to identify our business by the product or service we provide. I've talked about being in the asphalt paving business, the automobile business, the construction business, and the tax resolution business. But really, the business you're in is the value you provide to your customers, not necessarily the actual product or service.

Harvard Business School marketing professor Theodore Levitt told his students, "People don't want a quarter-inch drill. They want a quarter-inch hole." So companies that make hand tools may sell drills, but their business is holes. Levitt also said, "Kodak sells film, but they don't advertise film. They advertise memories." Charles Revson, the founder of Revlon, once said, "In the factory, we make cosmetics. In the drugstore, we sell hope."

In the tax representation business, our service involves doing a lot of things our customers don't really care about and would rather not have to deal with. In fact, one of the things that makes our job challenging is that it's not always easy to get our clients to give us the information we need so we can do what we promised. They'd rather avoid the unpleasant task of sorting through records and finding important documentation—in fact, I bet a substantial portion of our clients would rather have a root canal than do what we need them to do. Of course, we know that if everybody handled their tax obligations the way they're supposed to, they wouldn't need us, so we recognize that staying on top of our clients and even nagging them is part of what they're paying us to do. But our real business isn't about filling out forms, doing math calculations, analyzing financial information, and talking to IRS agents; our business is providing peace of mind and relief to our clients.

What's *your* business?

The Challenge of Target Marketing

Technology has made it easier than ever for most industries to identify market segments and target them. Once you know who your customers are, you can put together a plan to reach them by using media and other targeted methods. For example, when I was in the luxury automobile business, I found direct mail invitation sales events to be a very effective marketing strategy. Of course, I made sure that our message was delivered only to households above a certain income level because we knew those were the people who were more likely to buy our brand of car.

Ideally, you want to spend your marketing dollars reaching only individuals or companies that are your potential customers. It's a great goal, but in the real world, that's not always possible. Sometimes you have to market to a larger group to get to your customers.

As I mentioned, our market research indicates that about 6 percent of U.S. households are potential JK Harris & Company clients—that's the number of people who have a problem with overdue taxes. Unfortunately, I have no way of knowing who those people are until they call us. The IRS doesn't publish a list of them. In most other industries, identifying potential customers is easier. You may know, for example, that your typical customer lives in a certain area, or makes a particular amount of money, plays a certain sport, or is in a certain age group, or fits some other identifiable demographic. Our clients don't fit that type of profile. The only thing they all have in common is that they have delinquent tax issues they need help with.

"The word listen contains the same letters as the word silent."
—Alfred Brendel

So to identify prospective clients, we have to market to the entire population and wait for someone to respond to our message. Once they contact us, we can shift into a more targeted, traditional sales model where we identify needs, determine whether or not we can help, and, if we can, attempt to close the sale.

Don't let the idea that it's not always easy or even possible to do target marketing be an excuse for failing to try to do it. Target market as closely as you possibly can—to do it any other way is to waste money and reduce profits.

Know Your Customer

There are two angles to the issue of knowing your customer. One is to have a clear picture of your prospective customers. Who has a need for your product or service, is likely to buy it, and can afford it? For individuals, you'll want to know their demographics—how old they are, where they live, how much money they make, how many children and pets they have. For businesses, you need similar details—the industry, size of the company, location, number of employees, and so on.

Equally important is that you have a clear picture of your actual customers. How closely do the people who are actually buying from you resemble the prospective customer your marketing plan is targeting? If there's a match, your marketing plan is working. If you see a significant difference between your target market and the customers you have, you need to figure out the problem in your marketing strategy. Why are your marketing efforts working on a group you're not targeting? And what do you need to change—your strategy or your target market?

Another element to toss into this equation is this: How happy are you with your current customers? Do you want more of them? Or would you rather have customers with different characteristics—those who will buy more, not be so price-sensitive, or that will be easier to serve? You have to know who your customer is before you can decide whether to seek more customers who are similar or to put together a plan to go after a different customer group.

Don't have people buying from you without knowing who they are and why they're your customers.

Remember the Influencers

Consider the people who influence your customers' buying decisions as you develop your marketing plan. Advertising directed at children is the classic example. Toddlers, preschoolers, and elementary-aged children don't make purchases themselves, but advertisers spend millions targeting those kids because they know that youngsters can influence their parents' buying decisions. Similarly, you often see products designed for seniors being advertised in media that is targeted to baby boomers because the advertisers are hoping the baby boomers will either make the purchase for their parents or encourage their parents to buy whatever the item is for themselves. In business-to-business situations, the final decision-maker is typically influenced by a wide range of people, depending, of course, on the product or service involved.

We know we have clients who call us because a decision-influencer in their lives saw our ad and strongly suggested it. As

flashpoint

How Do Your Customers Make Their Buying Decisions?

A critical piece of knowledge for developing an effective marketing plan is to understand how your buyers make their buying decisions. What's important to them in the process? Does your customer make the decision alone, or are other people involved? Do they care about fancy presentations, or do they just want you to get to the bottom line?

When you understand these issues, you can develop a marketing plan that will take your customers through the buying process step by step in a way that's comfortable for them and profitable for you.

part of your marketing strategy, take the time to figure out who influences your customers and how you can best reach those people with your message.

Test, Measure, Roll Out, Measure, and Keep Measuring

Always test your marketing tactics before you roll them out on a full-scale basis. As I said when I was explaining Strategy 1, that's what allows you to keep your failures small and make your successes big.

The steps are simple: Test. Measure the results. Analyze the results. Decide if you need to make any changes. If you do, make them and test again. Let me repeat: If you make changes, you must test again—don't assume your changes will work. Once you're satisfied with the test results, you're ready to roll out. You have to gamble to a degree with your testing dollars, but don't spend any roll-out money until you know what your return will be.

Know Your Market, and Market Constantly

You'll never get to the point where you can stop measuring and testing your marketing. Just because a particular campaign was wildly successful once, twice, or even multiple times, doesn't mean it will always be successful. And just because something hasn't worked in the past doesn't mean it might not work in the future. For example, direct mail stopped working for us in 2001, so we stopped using it. We didn't test it again until 2006, and we discovered it was working again for us. We should have been testing it every year.

> *"Don't say you don't have enough time. You have exactly the same number of hours per day that were given to Helen Keller, Pasteur, Michaelangelo, Mother Teresa, Leonardo da Vinci, Thomas Jefferson, and Albert Einstein."*
>
> —H. Jackson Brown Jr.

The reason direct mail stopped working for us was that the IRS stopped placing tax liens on homes for an 18-month period, but we didn't realize that at the time. All we saw was that direct mail wasn't working. We did the right thing by stopping it, but we made a mistake by not retesting it sooner.

As technology advances and consumer habits change, you should always be considering new ways to market. Never shoot

Marketing vs. Advertising

To turn your company into a successful sales and marketing organization, be sure you know the difference between marketing and advertising. Advertising is paid messages in print, broadcast, or electronic media. Marketing is everything a company does to acquire and maintain customers, and includes advertising (usually the largest expense of a marketing plan), market research, public relations, pricing, distribution, customer service, sales, and community relations.

down a new idea just because what you're already doing is working fine. The new idea might work better. Reject it only after you're sure it won't work for you.

When it comes to direct response advertising, let the numbers make your decisions. If it's working, keep it up. If it's not working, stop it. Don't spend a lot of time trying to figure out why it isn't working. Most of the time, you're never going to know why one thing worked and something else didn't. Don't worry about that. Just do what works, and don't do what doesn't.

The Dangers of Direct Response Advertising

I am a huge fan of direct response advertising. It's the best type of advertising for most businesses, because it specifically asks the consumer to do something. The sole objective of every ad we run is to get someone to pick up the phone and call us or go to our website and contact us that way. We don't run institutional ads; I don't care about promoting the company except to our potential customers, and I want them to take action in response to our ads. If I'm going to spend money on ads, I want a direct payoff.

Successful direct response marketers are masters at pulling the emotional strings that will produce the results they want. They understand their market and what drives their customers' buying decisions. You can learn a lot about human nature just by studying direct response ads. They offer clear benefits (not just features), exclusivity (such as "available only through this special TV offer" and "others are imitations"), scarcity ("quantities are limited"), great prices ("regularly sold for three times as much"), special deals ("order now and get a second one free"), a sense of urgency ("call now; operators are standing by"), and security ("satisfaction guaranteed or your money back"). These are all elements that appeal to most people and it's an advertising strategy that works.

There's no debate that effective direct response advertising is very emotional. The advertiser knows that, with few exceptions, if people aren't motivated to take action while the ad is on, they probably won't do it later. Even direct response ads for simple kitchen or household gadgets have an emotional appeal—and therein lies the danger of this type of advertising. If your ads get too emotional, you could become the target of a state attorney general (AG) or other regulatory agency investigation.

While direct response advertising must be emotional, it's not always dramatic. The ads we run have a strong element of drama because we feature clients whom we've helped by solving their tax problems, and getting out from under a crushing tax debt is both dramatic and emotional. A kitchen gadget that helps you prepare healthy meals quickly doesn't lend itself to much drama in the ad, but it can be emotional when it appeals to your need to eat better and provide higher quality meals for your family. The key is to present the product and the offer in a way that prompts a response.

Unfortunately, there have been and will likely always be advertisers who don't just push the envelope, they cross the line. And when consumers start complaining that the product or service didn't live up to its pitch, that gets the attention of the AGs.

Whether or not you've actually done anything wrong, you'll find that being the target of an AG investigation is time-consuming, distracting, and punitively expensive because you not only have to pay your own attorneys, but you also have to reimburse the state for the hours their legal staff spent on the case. State consumer protection laws are weighted heavily in favor of the state. For example, you can be convicted of fraudulent advertising without a single consumer getting on the witness stand. All the state has to do is get an "expert" to say that a "reasonable consumer could" (not *would*) interpret the language of your ad to mean something misleading. You can offer hundreds or even thousands of people who would testify that your ads meant exactly what they said, and it doesn't matter. If someone could misinterpret it, you risk being convicted of fraudulent advertising.

Don't get the idea that false advertising charges are limited to fly-by-night operations that sell items like vitamins, weight-loss products, and get-rich-quick schemes. Dell is a company with a reputation for excellent products and great customer service, but the New York State Supreme Court found that some of its ads were fraudulent and misleading. In his decision in the case, Judge Joseph Teresi wrote that the company "engaged in repeated misleading, deceptive and unlawful business conduct, including false and deceptive advertising of financing promotions and the terms of warranties, fraudulent, misleading and deceptive practices in credit financing and failure to provide warranty service and rebates." Kellogg reached a settlement on federal charges that it falsely advertised the benefits for children of eating Frosted Mini-Wheats. Subway settled a false advertising case after some of the company's promotions for discounted food items weren't honored in all stores.

My point is that even well-meaning, reputable companies have had problems with their advertising and even honest mistakes can be expensive to deal with. This doesn't mean that you can't use some powerful advertising techniques—you just need to be careful.

Make Each Ad a Sales Call

The content of each one of your advertisements should be treated as a sales call and use well-honed selling skills. Don't wait until you're actually in front of a customer to start selling—if you take that approach, your ads won't be very effective. Every image, every word, and every bit of white space in your ad should have a purpose and work toward the goal of the ad, whether that's to make a sale or

"Early to bed, early to rise, work like hell, and advertise."

—Ed Turner (Ted Turner's father)

get the prospect to contact you so you can do a telephone or in-person sales presentation.

Measure your advertising messages against the psychology of persuasion discussed in Strategy 5 to be sure each ad contains the elements that will persuade a prospective customer to say yes to your offer.

Like a Dog with a Bone

You must be absolutely tenacious with your marketing. It's what drives sales, and sales are what drive your business. And that's why no matter how good—or bad—business is, you must always be marketing. When business is good, you need to keep feeding your customer pipeline. When business is bad, it will only get worse if you stop marketing.

When I bought my asphalt paving business, the previous owner had stopped marketing. The good news for me in that situation was that I was able to negotiate a much better price for the company, because all I was really buying was the equipment, not a reliable revenue stream. The company had no business. There were three or four small jobs on the books, and that was it—there was nothing in the pipeline. The owner could have commanded a much higher price if he had continued marketing and sold the company with some decent jobs that would have brought in some income.

The way a construction-related business markets is considerably different than how a consumer-oriented company markets, but it's nonetheless marketing. I didn't run ads, but I networked and promoted myself and my company. I learned how to subscribe to a construction industry reporting service to find out about jobs that were coming up in my market area. I learned which players were locked into relationships with which other players, so I knew which jobs were worth bidding on and which ones would be a waste of time. And I immediately joined and began actively participating in the local industry association and learned how to play the game by the unwritten rules.

Because the company had virtually no business when I bought it, I had no time to waste. I had to get as many jobs as I could, as fast as I could, to keep my crews working and to get the cash flowing in. I was selective about the jobs I bid on—I didn't bother to bid on jobs I knew I couldn't get because of their location or requirements, or because it was a known fact that the developer or the general contractor was locked into a relationship with another paving company. But because I needed the work to keep the doors open, I couldn't afford to get shopped on the jobs I did bid. I had to have every one of those jobs. So I decided on a potentially dangerous strategy: I knew what the going rate was and I undercut it by 25 to 35 cents a square yard (which is how asphalt paving is priced). It meant I had to run a lean operation so I didn't take a loss. But the market was good and there was plenty of construction work going on, so I got all the business I wanted that first year, and I put my company squarely on the playing field.

A key lesson I learned that year is that sometimes you have to buy your way into a market with lower prices. It's a valid marketing strategy. But your business can't be entirely about price because if it is, you'll lose market share to the next guy who comes along and undercuts you.

At JK Harris, we're tenacious about marketing. We study, analyze, test, and train our people—and we spend a lot of money. We buy more advertising during tax season than the rest of the year because we know that's when people who have tax debts are more inclined to do something about their problem, but we never relax our marketing efforts. That's a key reason why we're the industry leader.

Do You Need a Celebrity Spokesperson?

We live in a celebrity-obsessed culture. Big companies love the idea of having a celebrity spokesperson, and often more than one. In fact, being a product spokesperson can sometimes turn you into a celebrity. And some celebrities make a very nice living pitching various products. But will it help your business to have a celebrity touting your products?

Obviously, many companies think it will. Tiger Woods is a product-endorsement gold mine and plenty of other celebrities get paid millions of dollars to endorse every kind of product. The term used to describe the value of a celebrity spokesperson is *borrowed equity*, and the idea is that the celebrity's equity (value) will rub off on the brand being endorsed. But the brand only gets the borrowed equity for the time the spokesperson is under contract—and the borrowed equity isn't always what the brand had hoped for.

One of the more recent such cases is Michael Phelps, who was dropped by Kellogg's after he was photographed inhaling from a marijuana pipe. The Italian sneaker and tennis-gear company Tacchini was willing to pay tennis player Martina Hingis to endorse its products—until she sued it, claiming its gear was responsible for several injuries. And you almost have to feel sorry for the Beef Industry Council: After signing James Garner and Cybill Shepherd to endorsement deals in 1986, Garner had quadruple-bypass surgery (possibly from eating burgers and steaks) and Shepherd revealed that she doesn't eat meat. After that, the Beef Industry Council began using ordinary people in its commercials.

Another point to consider when you're using celebrities who are essentially their own brand is the question of whether you're building their brand or yours. Did Paris Hilton's commercial for Carl's Jr. increase burger sales or just Hilton's notoriety?

In 1999, I was introduced to Fran Tarkenton and hired him to speak at one of our company meetings. He was an excellent motivational speaker, a Hall of Fame football player, and very well-known. We were just starting to test television advertising and I decided to hire him as our spokesperson. I made it clear to him at the start that we couldn't afford a pricey endorsement deal, and he agreed to take stock options as compensation. We filmed some commercials and put them on the air. Those spots worked better than anything else we'd done to that point, and things were great. Then the second year rolled around, and Fran wanted the equity in the company, plus additional cash. I said no, and we immediately terminated our relationship.

We quickly created a generic replacement commercial that had no human in it, just words on the screen and the voice-over message: "If you're having tax problems, call this toll-free number." We couldn't stop advertising, because this was in January, and the first quarter of the year is our busiest time—we had to be out there in the public's view. (I'm sure Fran had that in mind when he made his demands.) While the generic spot was running, we got to work on a script and shot the first commercial that featured me. It took us about two months to get the new commercial done, and we got it on the air in March.

The generic spots did not pull as well as Fran's, and we were worried about how well the ones featuring me would do. After all, nobody knew me. We were hoping the ads with me would at least do better than the generic ones, but we were totally unprepared for what happened. As soon as the new commercials started running, we started setting records for calls and appointments. We were blowing all our previous performance records away. My commercials were pulling 30 percent more calls than Fran's had done the previous year—and we thought his performed well!

We learned a very important lesson, which was that we didn't need expensive outside talent to promote our business. I just told our story. I told people that if they had a problem with the IRS, we could help them. Then, in addition to me, we started adding some of our consultants to the commercials.

> "The Golden Rule for every business man is this: Put yourself in the customer's place."
> —Orison Swett Marden

These are real people that you might end up meeting with if you call us. Not only are we not celebrities, it's obvious we're not actors. But people trust those commercials, they believe what we're saying, and they call—which is what we want to happen.

Most companies would be wise to take any money they might pay to a celebrity for an endorsement and invest that in developing some really creative ideas that will make them stand out and establish their own brand—not the celebrity—in the consumer's mind.

Put Your Money Where Your Mouth Is

Stand behind your products with some type of money-back guarantee—and don't make it impossible for your customers to get their money back if they want it.

When I bought the tax representation business manual from Jack McDonough, I was a little hesitant. He claimed his plan was tested, proven, and perfected—all I had to do was put it into operation. How did I know for sure that it would really work? I couldn't know until I purchased the product and tried it. Jack dealt with that by offering a money-back guarantee. If I wasn't satisfied, I could send his manual back within 30 days and get all of my money back.

Will there be times when people will take advantage of your refund policy? Probably. I could have photocopied Jack's manual and returned it, gotten my money back, and still used his information. But I don't do things like that—and the vast majority of people don't, either. But his refund policy gave me the comfort level I needed to make the investment in his product. If you don't trust your own product to perform, how can your customers? By the way, Jack's program worked far better for me than he predicted.

Create a clear, consistent, easy-to-apply return or refund policy; incorporate it into your marketing message; and make sure everyone who deals with customers knows what it is so it can be consis-tently honored.

Change with the Times

Just because a particular marketing strategy works, don't assume it will always work. When JK Harris & Company was launched, we spent 100 percent of our advertising dollars on newspaper—noth-ing on television, and certainly not a dime on the internet. Today, less than 5 percent of our advertising budget is allocated to print; the rest is spent on television, radio, and internet advertising. Online, we buy pay-per-clicks and we invest in search engine opti-mization (SEO), search engine marketing (SEM), and online repu-tation management (ORM). By the way, you don't have to be a technical whiz, but you need to understand those terms and get people on your team who know how to develop and implement effective SEO, SEM, and ORM strategies, as well as stay current with new developments.

SEO refers to improving the volume or quality of traffic from search engines to a website through natural or organic search results, not paid results. As you develop your SEO plan, you have to consider how search engines work and what people search for. Optimizing a website primarily involves managing its content and HTML codes to increase its relevance to specific keywords and search terms and to remove barriers to the indexing activities of search engines. One of the challenges of SEO is that the search engines routinely change their algorithms to stay a step ahead of the online marketers who try to manipulate them. But even if you don't do any online selling, it's a good idea to have a website that's search engine-friendly.

Search engine marketing is a bigger ball game. Like SEO, the goal of SEM is to increase website traffic, but it does it through a combination of SEO plus paid placements (typically pay-per-click), contextual advertising (ads related to the content of the website), and paid inclusion (where you pay the search engine company to include your site on search results).

Online reputation management is, as the name implies, paying attention to and managing your company's internet reputation, which is what people are saying about your company and your products and services online. Effective ORM requires careful monitoring, swift response to negative items (the response will vary depending on the specific item), and proactive steps to positively influence public perception.

Less than a decade ago, SEM, SEO, and ORM weren't even in our vocabulary, much less part of our marketing plans. Today, they're almost old news. Social and business networking sites, Twitter, mobile communications, and more all need to be considered in your marketing strategy.

You also need to consider evolving social customs and public perception. For example, it wasn't that long ago that no television network would have accepted a commercial advertising a drug for erectile dysfunction. Today, you probably know their slogans and jingles whether or not you're a prospective user. When we first launched our tax resolution service, nobody was advertising this business on television, and even the print advertising was limited. A lot of people thought we were actually the IRS trying to set them up in a sting-type operation—and yes, that made it really tough to get people to give us enough information so we could decide if we could do anything for them. Today, thanks largely to advertising and other marketing efforts, the public recognizes that when they have issues with a tax collection agency at the federal or state level, they have resources. The social customs and public perception have changed, and marketing methods have changed as well.

Always be looking forward with your marketing strategy. Don't wait until something completely stops working to look for an alternative. And don't miss out on a great opportunity because you weren't paying attention.

Market with Great Customer Service

Customers buy products and services to gain the benefits promised by them. If your customers decide that either you can't deliver the benefits, or it's too much trouble to deal with you to get the benefits, they'll go somewhere else. On the other hand, if your customers like your products and the way you treat them, they're going to tell people, and that will bring more business your way. This is another piece of basic business advice that is all too often ignored. And it's why you need to constantly be looking at your operation through the eyes of your customers and providing top-notch customer service.

It's not hard to forget to consider the customer's perspective and get wrapped up in doing what's easiest and best for you. It's also easy to write customers off as too demanding, unreasonable, and even unrealistic. But those customers have voices, and if they're unhappy, they will make their voices heard in a variety of ways.

In a relatively new industry, when you don't have a lot of competition, you might be able to get away with offering mediocre or even poor customer service. Or when the economy is booming and there's so much business out there that it doesn't matter if you make your customers mad, you can still make money even if you let customer service slide. But when the competition gets tough and the economy contracts, your customer service will set you apart and give you an edge. Don't wait until that happens to figure out how to deliver the service that keeps your customers coming back and referring others to you. This is another lesson we learned in the school of hard knocks.

In the early days of JK Harris & Company, we weren't as customer oriented as we should have been. In fact, a colleague of mine who eventually joined the company told me, "You don't think like a regular customer service–oriented type of business. You think like the IRS. You think that the clients *have* to come to you because they have nowhere else to go. You think they need you more than you need them."

He was right. And in the beginning, it was true—our clients needed us because they had no other real alternative. Sure, some CPAs and attorneys did tax resolution work, but our typical client couldn't afford their fees. Our clients weren't likely to leave us. We were getting the work done, and we figured holding the customer's hand through the process wasn't necessary.

We were so wrong.

I've told you that we had been the target of investigations by a group of 18 attorneys general, which were prompted in large part by consumer complaints. The IRS investigation didn't help matters, but the AGs were primarily focused on the consumer issues. When we reviewed the complaints the AGs had received, reading the files and checking to see exactly what we did, we realized that in a majority of the cases, we were absolutely right, we had done exactly what we promised, and had achieved the best possible resolution for the clients on their tax issues. We didn't feel we owed those customers a refund, but when we showed the documentation to the AGs, they almost always sided with the consumer.

We realized that all too often the view a customer has of a company's performance is based on perception, not reality. Our employees are good, decent people who care about our clients and who want to do a good job for them. Our fees are fair and usually significantly lower than what CPAs, attorneys, and even other tax resolution firms would charge for the same work. But all of that doesn't matter if the client's perception is different from the reality. What we figured out was that the people who do what we refer to as our production work—completing the tax returns, analyzing the client's situation, negotiating with the IRS—are accountants who are basically number-crunchers and think that the Internal Revenue Code is more exciting than any bestselling novel. They are typically not "people" people. They're not good at translating financial and tax issues into language a nonaccountant would understand. In fact, most of them would prefer not to interact with people much at all, which is why they would avoid doing things like returning telephone calls and making the clients feel comfortable with what we were doing for them.

Because we were the leader in the industry, we were getting away with treating our customers with less than the total respect and consideration they deserved—and not because we intentionally *wanted* to treat them poorly but because the people whose job it was to deliver customer service were focused on the production side of their work and not the people. We should have taken a lesson from that 1970s song by the Carpenters and realized that, like the birds and Karen Carpenter, customers "long to be close to you."

We weren't listening. There's an old story that has a number of variations, but basically it's about a farmer who buys a mule, but he can't get the mule to do what he wants. So he goes back to the guy he bought the mule from and says, "This mule is worthless. You need to take him back." The mule's seller asks for a chance to take a look at the mule and see if he can fix the problem. He goes out to the farm, looks the mule over carefully, then picks up a two by four and hits the mule in the head as hard as he can. The mule is clearly stunned, and the farmer is shocked. He demands, "What are you trying to do? Kill him?" "No," said the man. "With this mule, you just have to get his attention."

Our company was growing at an impressive rate, but we hadn't yet been hit with the proverbial two by four. And then we were—not once, but twice.

One was the AG investigations. Even though most of the complaints received by the AGs were without any merit, we still had to deal with them, and that was time-consuming and expensive. The second hit was that it didn't take long for a bunch of competitors to enter the market and for our customers to realize that they had a choice. We paid a price for our attitude. It was an expensive lesson, but we've learned it well, and we won't make it again. Always put yourself in the customer's shoes. It's a place we should have been from the beginning.

Our focus on customer service has not only reduced the number of complaints we receive, it has increased the amount of positive feedback from clients. Those compliments have increased the pride our employees feel in their jobs and their performance. Their supervisor can tell them they're doing a great job and that's

> "What matters is not what you say but what people hear."
> —Frank Luntz

good, but when they hear it from a customer, that's special and very motivating.

Communication Is Critical

You may know that you have everything under control, but if you don't take the time to tell your customer, you've got a problem.

Back in the 1980s, an Eastern Airlines plane lost an engine shortly after take-off from Miami International Airport. By "lost," I mean the engine fell off the plane. It took a great deal of skill for the pilot to safely return the aircraft to the airport. Later, some of the passengers complained that the pilot didn't keep them well enough informed about what was happening during the emergency. The pilot's response was, "I was busy flying the plane!"

More recently, U.S. Airway's pilot Chesley B. "Sully" Sullenberger III only told his passengers to "brace for impact" before he splash-landed into New York's Hudson River. I'm sure he had plenty to say to the various air traffic controllers who were managing the air space as he assessed the damage to the aircraft and made his decision about what to do, but he didn't talk to the passengers.

In the life-and-death aspect of those situations, the fact that pilots didn't take the time to chat with the passengers until the plane was safely on the ground in the Eastern Airlines case or until the passengers were off the plane and on rescue vessels in the U.S. Airways situation was understandable. But in most business situations, there's no excuse for failing to communicate with your customers. What's more, most customers will accept whatever problems you're having if you'll just keep them informed.

This was another hard-learned lesson for us. Our case specialists know that dealing with the IRS is a long, drawn-out process, and sometimes it can take months for things to happen. But our clients don't know that. When we aren't communicating with them, they think we're not working on their case. Remember,

Eliminate Your Customer Service Department

We don't have a customer service department. We believe that we must be our clients' advocate, so we have a client advocacy department that's overseen by our executive vice president of client advocacy. And it isn't just semantics or a clever, feel-good thing. Our job is to go to bat for the client, whether it's with the IRS, another tax collection entity, or even with someone else in our own company. This goes beyond basic customer service, as important as that is. An advocate is someone who argues for a cause, who pleads on another's behalf. Everyone in our organization is an advocate for the client. Everyone. Period.

perception is what counts. Now we contact them on a regular basis, even if all we do is tell them we don't have any news to tell them.

Something else we've done is ask our customers how they want to be communicated with. We have so many options today—phone, e-mail, snail mail, fax, and so on. We find out which communication methods our customers prefer, and use them.

We also encourage our case specialists to get to know their customers as people rather than file numbers. If, for example, a case specialist happens to be talking to a customer and notices from the information in the file that the customer has a birthday coming up, the case specialist will offer good wishes. It's all part of good, strong communications.

Enforce Customer Service Rules

Of course, you should enforce all the rules you have—otherwise, why have them? But it is especially important that you enforce the rules regarding good customer service.

As I've said, we have had people who were great at doing the work behind the service, but they didn't like dealing directly with clients, and so they avoided it. They would do almost anything to get out of answering phones and returning calls. We had rules about that, but the rules weren't being enforced.

I ended up reorganizing the business and putting an enforcer over that department, someone who understood the importance of customer service, who inspects what he expects, and who doesn't let people get away with doing less than what's required. The customer is more important than the comfort zone of our employees.

There's Just No Pleasing Some People

One of the most frustrating aspects of being in business is the customer you can't please, no matter what you do. The nature of our business and our typical client makes our customer relationships more challenging than many other types of ventures, but every company has the impossible-to-please customers. We've had clients for whom we have provided our full service *and* refunded 100 percent of their fees, and they've still filed a complaint against us. I think that's because the vast majority of our clients are procrastinators, and procrastinators don't like to accept responsibility. They have to blame someone else for their mistakes.

The only way to deal with these customers is to document everything so you're prepared for any potential fallout, do the best you can, and move on. Don't engage a customer who attacks you unfairly. If the customer has a legitimate complaint, do everything you can to make it right. But if the customer is being unreasonable, don't stoop to his level—no matter how tempted you may be.

There will always be customers who try to rip you off. Retailers see this all the time with shoplifters and fraudulent returns. B2B operations have their share of customers who think they're entitled to something for nothing. And it's no surprise that in the tax resolution

> *"Even if you're on the right track, you'll get run over if you just sit there."*
>
> —Will Rogers

business, where we're dealing with procrastinators who owe back taxes to the IRS, some of them actually try to avoid paying us for our services. Some of them even get help from unexpected sources, such

Crisis Management

Every company should have a crisis management plan in place before you need it. I didn't realize that in 2000 when we were raided by the IRS, and in my response, I did a lot of things wrong, the company suffered some devastating blows, and we missed some tremendous opportunities.

Our company has since retained Jonathan Bernstein of Bernstein Crisis Management in Sierra Madre, California, and he has taught us how to deal with situations like that, as well as routine negative publicity generated by consumer complaints. Jonathan defines a crisis as any situation that's threatening or could threaten to harm people or property, seriously interrupt business, damage reputation, or negatively impact share value. The IRS raid clearly qualified as a crisis. So did the AG investigations. And on a smaller scale, we treat complaints posted about us on the internet as crises because they have the potential to damage our reputation and negatively impact share value.

Jonathan explains it this way: He says that the routine function of marketing is to *build* the value of the business. The crisis communications function of marketing is to *preserve* the value of the business.

The key to effective crisis management is to recognize the opportunity and get out in front of it, not to try to hide. But your statements and other responses need to be orchestrated by someone who understands consumer psychology and can work with your attorneys to keep you safe from a legal standpoint while getting your message out to your customers, stakeholders, and the general public.

as when, during our first year in business, we prepared and submitted an offer in compromise for a client who had paid us half of the fee and was to pay the balance when the IRS accepted the offer. As soon as he found out the offer was going to be accepted, he contacted the IRS revenue officer, who told him he could fire us and sign the offer agreement, which he promptly did.

Sometimes the customer is the problem. Deal with it.

Public Opinion Counts

Managing your public relations is part art, part science, and totally essential. Many of the strategies are evolving with technology, which is why you need a PR expert guiding you.

When we were about a year and a half old, I retained a public relations firm that did a great job for us. One of the most valuable things the firm did was get the *Wall Street Journal* to write an article about us. That article, published in 1999, said, "Today J. K. Harris . . . has become far and away the most successful tax-resolution company." We began using that quote in our ads and other marketing materials immediately, and we still use it today. It was true then, and it's even truer now. But what really gives the statement credibility is the fact that it was published in the *Wall Street Journal*—we didn't say it, the reporter wrote it after he did his research. It's an independent statement from a reputable source. If you're fortunate enough to have something similar said about your company, take advantage of it.

But in 2000, after we were raided by the IRS, I shut down all our publicity efforts. I'd heard that any publicity is good publicity. You've probably heard the saying: I don't care what you say about me as long as you're talking about me and you spell my name right. I'm not sure I agree with that theory, and I wasn't about to test it. We were getting some news coverage because of the raid and subsequent investigation, but it wasn't good. I decided the safest thing to do was stop trying to get publicity. As it turned out, that was a mistake. I went under the radar when what I should have been doing was countering all the negative publicity with positive publicity.

Of course, hindsight is always 20/20. If I had had a PR firm with crisis management expertise when the raid happened, they would have advised me to go on the offense, and I would have listened. I would have continued my positive PR campaign and added a strategy to deal with the negative information.

The internet has revolutionized the way smart companies handle PR. Once a story gets on the internet, it's going to be there forever. Customer complaints posted on the internet—valid or not—don't go away. And even local news items are now available for anyone in the world to see.

The best and simplest online PR strategy you can use is to remember that it's a numbers game. You just have to get more positive content out there than whatever negative information is being generated about you. And you need to do it in a way that the positive content shows up higher in search engine results than the negative. You don't have to personally understand meta tags, keywords, or algorithms—but you have to get people on your team who do.

It took us several years to realize just how damaging a bad online reputation can be. In the early 2000s, we didn't recognize how fast internet use was growing and how often people were doing online searches to get information about companies before doing business with them—and we weren't alone. A lot of good companies with smart marketing departments dropped the ball on that one.

We have since hired one of the best firms in the country to help us with our search engine positioning. They do a great job, but this isn't a fix-it-and-forget-it process. It's a constant battle. Google and the other search engines don't want users to be able to manipulate their results, so they keep changing their algorithms so that what you did a few months ago to get your positive information at the top of the search results won't work now.

We also have two full-time people who do nothing but monitor what's said about JK Harris on the internet and make an appropriate response. If it's a customer service issue, we deal with it. We also post positive articles, answer questions on discussion boards, post comments on blogs, and so on so content is crawled by the search engines and shows up in search results.

When it comes to a company's reputation, the internet is a double-edged sword. On the one hand, it's a great way for a business to get its message out, to tell people what it can do, and even to make sales. On the other hand, anybody with a gripe—legitimate or not—can post a negative comment about any business, and there's very little you can do to have those complaints removed, and often you can't even respond to them. In fact, for a number of reasons, it's not a good idea to make a specific response online to a complaint even if the site allows it. Legitimate complaints should be addressed privately, between you and your customer, not in a public forum. This is especially true when you provide a professional service such as ours, where we deal with confidential financial information. If you're not able to resolve the complaint—and face it, as I've already said, every company is going to have customers you just can't make happy—the customer will only keep repeating the negative information and that will drive the page ranking of the site up. Don't get into an online spitting contest with an unhappy customer.

Google and the other search engines are trying to put safeguards in place so that decent companies aren't unfairly maligned. The search engines are aware that some people put up these so-called "consumer" sites and will take money from companies to not post negative information about them. If you have complaints about your company posted on a site and you think that's what's happening, file complaints with the search engines. If Google and the other search engines determine the site isn't a legitimate consumer site, they'll blacklist it so it doesn't come up in the search engine results. What's most important is to remember that this takes constant vigilance on your part. You have to stay on top of it.

——— KEY LESSONS ———

⁕ *Know your market inside and out, from every angle.* In addition to knowing your customers, know what and who influences their decisions. Know your competitors, and be aware of all circumstances that can impact your market.

⁕ *Seek out industry experts who can help with your marketing efforts.* Be willing to pay for their advice; it's a good investment for your company.

⁕ *Market research is an ongoing process.* Don't do it in the beginning and assume your market will never change, because it will. Keep studying it so you can stay ahead of any changes.

⁕ *Be realistic with your interpretation of your market analysis.* Accept the facts as they are, not how you wish they were.

⁕ *Know what business you are actually in.* It's not the product or service you offer, it's the value you provide to your customers.

⁕ *Engage in extremely targeted marketing whenever possible.* While it can't always be avoided, don't waste any more money than you absolutely have to marketing to people who aren't your potential customers or who can't influence your customers.

⁕ *Know how your customers make their buying decisions and tailor your marketing efforts to appeal to that process.*

⁕ *Never stop testing and measuring.* Test any marketing idea before you roll it out. If you don't get the results you want, make adjustments and test again. Don't spend money on a full roll-out for something you aren't sure will work. And measure routinely so you know if the effectiveness of a particular strategy has either increased or decreased. If it's increased, you may want to do more of it. If it's decreased, stop it and find something else that works.

✳ *Make your advertising messages strong and truthful.* Certainly your ads need to be persuasive, but they can't be misleading or fraudulent.

✳ *Market continuously.* Whether business is up or down, you need to always be feeding the marketing pipeline.

✳ *You probably don't need a celebrity spokesperson.* Hiring a celebrity to pitch your product can be expensive, and the payoff isn't always worth it. Invest in creative ideas that will make you and your brand stand out instead.

✳ *Guarantee your product*, and make that guarantee part of your marketing message.

✳ *If you're creating a new company, or even a new division or subsidiary of your existing company, choose a name that will have marketing impact.* It should identify what you do, be memorable and clever, and be easy to pronounce.

✳ *Stay out of ruts.* Incorporate the latest technologies into your marketing strategy. Don't ignore something just because you don't understand it; find someone who does and who can figure out if it can help you.

✳ *Use customer service as a marketing tool.* Word-of-mouth marketing is extremely powerful and the best way to generate that kind of buzz is through outstanding customer service.

✳ *Communicate with your customers.* Whether the news is good or bad, don't let them feel like they're being left in the dark.

Make everyone a customer advocate. Create a culture where the customer comes first, and everyone knows that.

Recognize that you'll have difficult customers. There are some people who just won't be happy, no matter what you do. It's OK to refer those people to your competitors.

Put a crisis prevention and management plan in place before you need it. Don't allow yourself to be blindsided by a situation that could harm your people or property, interrupt your business, or damage your reputation. If you think it can't happen to you, you're wrong.

Respect the strength of public opinion and manage your reputation accordingly.

Recognize the impact the internet has had on marketing and public relations. Make a substantial investment in managing your online image, and make it an ongoing process.

Build a Sales Team That Can Really Sell

My product or service is so good it sells itself.

Bull #%*$! That statement is one of the biggest lies ever told. Nothing sells itself.

If something could "sell itself," how would you find out about it to begin with? Somebody would have to tell you about it, or you would have to see an ad or an article or some other piece of literature about it, and that's part of the sales and marketing process.

No product is so good or so necessary that it can survive in the marketplace without a sales effort to support it. You can build all the better mousetraps you want, but the world will not beat a path to your door unless you make the effort to sell your mousetraps.

Another point to remember is that if you do have something great, other people are going to try to come up with their own version of it. Yours may be better, but if the other guy is actively selling his and you're letting yours "sell itself," who do you think is going to make the sale?

The really good news here is that this means even products and services that are not absolutely top-of-the-line, essential, or even particularly distinctive can be very profitable—if you use strong marketing and sales strategies. If you need proof, consider the story of Oracle.

When Larry Ellison founded Oracle in 1977, he had a database product that didn't work. You couldn't use it to add 1 plus 1 and get 2, because you could run that query and get 3, then run it again a few minutes later and get 6. The product wasn't functional, and it should never have been sold. Yet today, that same database that didn't work is the flagship product for the world's largest business software company.

At the time Ellison launched Oracle, there were two other database companies in business with products that actually

What Is Salesmanship?

The fundamentals of selling haven't changed since commerce began. In *Overnight Success*, a biography of FedEx founder Frederick Smith by Vance Trimble, Smith's father was quoted as saying: "This was a matter of salesmanship—as all things are. In this instance it was a matter of making others see through my eyes, of influencing them to adopt my viewpoint. Some salesmen put the proposition to the customer on the ground of charity, others beg assistance to make up their quota, and some actually talk hard luck at home. This system is all wrong. Any fellow who talks like that is no salesman. The man who gets the business is an honest, sincere, intelligent, modest man who knows when to stop talking to his prospect as well as when to begin. . . . A salesman must learn to know without being told what his prospect really desires."

worked. But those companies were run by engineers who were perfectionists. They wanted to create the absolute best database possible. They wanted their software to work flawlessly before taking it to market. That's an admirable goal, but it's not practical in today's world.

Back in the '80s, Oracle users were some of the loudest bashers of the company and its product. They hated the product and predicted failure for the company. And yet, Oracle has come out on top, and of the two other companies that might have been its competition in the beginning, one doesn't exist today and the other is a very small niche player in the market.

So how did Larry Ellison take his substandard, unreliable product, hit the flashpoint, and win the battle of the databases? He did it by concentrating on sales and marketing.

What Larry Ellison knew, and what we all need to learn and remember, is that it doesn't matter how good your product or service is. Especially when you're in a new industry, but always when you are fighting for market share, what counts is who's out there doing the best job at marketing and selling the product.

Ellison knew his product was absolutely every negative thing the users said about it, and probably worse. He wasn't happy about that, and he had his partners working on it to improve it, but it wasn't even close to what the competition was offering. Instead of waiting for the fixes to happen, he went out and sold his product, primarily to the government. He knew the problems would eventually be fixed, but he also knew he couldn't wait for that to happen before he sold the product and established his position in the marketplace. That first Oracle database that didn't work couldn't sell itself, but neither could the databases that were on the market at the time that *did* work.

> *"If Bill Gates had a dime for every time Windows crashed . . . oh, wait! He already does!"*
> —Unknown

Products and services don't sell themselves. People sell products and services, and their success is dependent on their sales skills.

A note to keep in mind as you read about this strategy: Though in many places I use the words *product* and *service* almost interchangeably, there are distinct differences in how you sell tangibles and intangibles. Adapt any sales advice to your particular operation.

The Sales and Marketing Partnership

Though we often say "salesandmarketing" as though it were one word, sales and marketing are actually separate functions that need to be fully integrated to produce the results you want. Marketing is what you do to reach potential customers with your message so that they'll be receptive to your sales efforts. The sales process is the interpersonal interaction that closes the sale. Sales and marketing must be in concert to be effective.

The challenge is that these two teams don't always play nice with each other. Salespeople complain about not getting sufficient support from marketing, and marketing people complain about being underappreciated by sales and underpaid compared to sales based on their contribution to the process. Both sides can be quick to blame the other when revenue drops.

The solution is to cultivate a cooperative relationship between these two efforts and the people involved. Remind them regularly that they are all on the same team, working for the same company, with (we hope) the same goals.

Your sales team needs to know exactly what's happening in your marketing efforts. They need to see the ads, the news releases, know when the website has been updated, and so on. They should never be caught off guard by not knowing what's being said in all your public communications. And since your marketing team should be tracking what the competition is doing, they should be sharing that with the sales staff as well. Make it mandatory that they spend time with each other. Let salespeople contribute ideas to marketing, and require marketing people to periodically spend time in the field with salespeople. And make sure everybody gets credit when credit is due.

Can Anyone Learn to Sell?

I'm a huge proponent of continuing education, and I believe companies have a responsibility to make training available to their employees. When you do that, you enhance the employees' skills, make them more valuable to your operation, and increase their loyalty, which reduces turnover. It's definitely a worthwhile investment.

Just about anyone can learn selling skills—you can learn to ask questions, listen to the answers, read body language, and guide people to a solution for their problems that includes purchasing your product or service. How well you'll actually do it out there in the real world depends on how suited your personality is to sales.

In Strategy 3, I told you about JK Harris's first sales team—a group of really great people, but three-fourths of them simply weren't cut out to be in sales. I tried, but I couldn't solve that problem with training. You can teach a dog all the tricks in the world, but you can't teach it to be a cat. I wasn't going to be able to teach people who should never have been in sales in the first place to be good salespeople, much less great ones. So just a couple of years after the company started, I had to replace all but about 25 percent of our sales consultants.

It's not that the people I had to let go were bad people. It's not that they didn't work hard. They just didn't have the personalities that would incline them to be sales superstars—and I wanted all superstars on my team, and so should you. Many of the people I had to let go probably could have stayed in the sales profession, made an adequate living, and do well enough with another company to avoid getting fired for poor performance. But they wouldn't have been happy. Consciously or not, they knew they weren't the best fit for a sales job. They needed to find careers that were better suited to their personalities.

You've probably heard about the 80/20 rule, also known as Pareto's Principle. This dates back to 1906, when Italian economist Vilfredo Pareto observed that 20 percent of the people held 80 percent of the wealth in Italy. It has evolved into a common rule of thumb in business—80 percent of your revenue comes from 20 percent of your customers, 80 percent of the work is done by 20 percent of the workers, 80 percent of your sales are made by 20 percent of your salespeople, and so on.

If you use whole person assessments as a hiring tool with your sales team, you can toss the 80/20 rule out the window when it comes to sales performance—any performance, for that matter. I believe the reason we see the 80/20 rule working in sales is because the vast majority of companies don't screen candidates to see if they have a true sales personality. They're putting people who should be working as something else into sales positions. Now, it's true that anyone who wants to learn selling skills can learn them. In fact, I recommend that everyone take the time to learn basic sales skills, because knowing and using those skills can benefit you in all your human interactions.

But just because you know how to play the piano doesn't mean you can be a concert pianist. Just because you know how to rhyme words doesn't mean you can be a great poet. And just because you know the skills involved in selling doesn't mean you have the natural aptitude. When it comes to sales, the skills are fairly easy to learn, but you either have the personality or you don't. You either love doing it or you don't. And if you don't, you might be a competent salesperson, but you'll never be a superstar.

Don't hire salespeople whose maximum achievement is likely to be merely competent. Where is that going to take your company?

In the beginning, we hired almost everybody who applied for a sales position. We were growing so fast we had the openings, and people were coming to us who were my family members as well as family members and friends of the sales consultants who were already on board. If they had some sales experience and we liked them, we'd hire them.

Today, because of our extensive screening process, we hire maybe 2 percent of the people who apply for sales positions. And even with that screening, we still have turnover. Screening can identify the people who have the natural inclination and ability, but it can't provide the motivation. So when we hire people who don't perform well, or whose performance falls into the bottom 10 to 20 percent of the group and stays there, we replace them.

Is that harsh? I don't think so. Salespeople who aren't doing a good job generally aren't any happier with their own performance than you are. You're doing them and your company a favor by encouraging them to move into a position where they can do better.

The Most Important Selling Skill

The right personality is important but your sales team still needs to be trained in product knowledge and skilled in sales techniques.

I've studied numerous sales training curriculums and what I find lacking in most of them is the teaching of the psychology of persuasion. Salespeople need to understand why people buy the things they buy and how they make their buying decisions.

When you're selling something, whether it's your company's product or you're trying to convince your spouse to agree with you on a vacation destination, your goal is to get people to say yes. And you do this by using the psychology of persuasion. Salespeople who use the psychology of persuasion flourish; those who don't will find other occupations.

The key here, though, is persuasion, *not* manipulation. People can usually sense when they're being manipulated, and they don't like it. Manipulation is an attempt at controlling the other person, essentially getting him to do something because you want him to, not to do it on his own volition. What we tend to think of as high-pressure sales tactics are typically manipulation not persuasion. Sales achieved through manipulation are likely to get canceled; customers obtained through manipulation are likely to file complaints. It's just not worth it. By contrast, customers who have been persuaded are doing business with you because they want to, not because you tricked them into it. Persuasion is an attempt to influence someone while still treating him as a responsible individual capable of making his own decisions

In *Influence: The Psychology of Persuasion*, Robert B. Cialdini explains what he calls the weapons of influence—reciprocation, commitment and consistency, social proof, liking, authority, and scarcity. Let's take a brief look at each one.

RECIPROCATION

Consider this scenario: You're entering a building with an exterior door and an interior door. Someone else gets to the exterior door slightly ahead of you and holds the door open for you. You step to the interior door, and what do you do? You hold the door for the person who just held it for you. That's reciprocation. When you create a feeling of indebtedness, you create an automatic response of yes. Do something for someone, and he or she will feel obligated to repay you.

That's one of the reasons product samples are such an effective sales tool. Not only does the customer actually touch and taste the product, but he has received a gift that he now feels he must reciprocate—and he does that by purchasing. The same principle applies when a charity sends you "free" return address labels or some other token. You're told you're welcome to keep the gift without obligation, but then you're urged to make a donation. Obviously the tactic works, because charities keep on using it.

Another way to apply this strategy is to ask for more than what you really want or expect, then ask for what you want. If you get what you first ask for, great. But if you don't, you're ideally positioned to get what you really want. Cialdini tells the story of being approached by a youngster who was selling tickets to an upcoming Boy Scouts circus. Cialdini declined, and the boy countered by asking if he would buy some chocolate bars instead. Cialdini bought two of the overpriced candy bars, even though he didn't like them. He didn't realize why at the time, but the event

Another Way to Use Reciprocation

Here's another way to use reciprocation that doesn't necessarily apply to a sales situation. In social psychology, reciprocity refers to responding to a positive action with another positive action, and responding to a negative action with another negative one. So let's say you're the customer and the service you're getting is leaving a lot to be desired. You could complain about the lousy service, but that's probably not going to get you much more than an apology from a supervisor. Instead, try thanking the person you're dealing with for the great job he's doing.

You know he's not doing a great job. He may or may not realize he's not doing a great job. But you've just paid him a compliment, and it's human nature to respond to something nice that's said about us by trying to be more of whatever that is. So in most cases, when you tell someone who isn't doing a particularly good job that you appreciate what he's doing, he'll reciprocate by trying harder.

drove him to figure it out: We tend to view the second request as a concession to which we feel obligated to reciprocate.

COMMITMENT AND CONSISTENCY

Once someone has made a personal commitment, the pressure to be consistent with that commitment is tremendous. Cialdini writes, "Once a stand is taken, there is a natural tendency to behave in ways that are stubbornly consistent with the stand."

The most effective way to use this strategy is to start small and move up. Ask people to make commitments about apparently minor things and then gently guide them to a greater commitment that will result in the sale. After small commitments have been made, people tend to add justifications to support those commitments and are willing to commit themselves even further.

Our sales consultants used to ask our customers for a commitment to the entire tax resolution package during their first meeting. We've found a strategy that's far more effective for us and more palatable for our customers, which is to use a multi-part process and let the customer commit in increasing degrees as he goes along. We know that the customer has a problem and needs our help—if he didn't, he wouldn't be in our office. That's the first small commitment. Next, our sales consultants explain how our services work: We first get the customer's past-due tax returns filed (also known as getting the client in compliance) and figure out exactly how much he owes; next we analyze his situation, determine the best approach to take with the IRS, and make our recommendation; then we implement that recommendation. The customer is asked to only purchase the first step of getting his tax returns current and determining a resolution strategy, which is the next small commitment, with the understanding that if he's satisfied with the results of that step, he'll move to the implementation step. With each commitment, the customer becomes more confident in his decision to contact and then hire us and demonstrates behaviors that are consistent with that decision up to and including committing to the final step of the process.

SOCIAL PROOF

When someone smiles at you, it's hard to do anything except smile back. In any situation when we're not sure what to do, we look to see what others are doing to help us decide. The behavior of others provides justification or proof of the validity of our own decisions. That's why JK Harris & Company uses "the nation's largest tax resolution firm" in our advertising—from a sales perspective, the fact that so many people turn to us when they have a problem with the IRS is proof that they're doing the right thing. That's why testimonials are such a powerful advertising tool. And it's why "rebellious" teenagers all seem to dress alike.

Top salespeople are always prepared with social proof to encourage their prospects to say yes as well as to validate a positive buying decision.

LIKING

How many times have you done something you didn't particularly want to do, but you did it because someone you like asked you to? Top salespeople learn the persuasion techniques that reinforce likeability—even though they may not be particularly likeable—which makes it easier for customers to decide to buy from them.

Products sold through home parties are the best evidence of how liking—as well as the other weapons of influence—work. The hostess invites her friends and co-workers to a party where kitchen gadgets, jewelry, clothes, home décor, candles, and even wine will be sold. The guests may have absolutely no interest in the products, but they accept the invitation because they like the hostess. Once at the party, you'll see reciprocation demonstrated when games are played, prizes are awarded, and refreshments served. Then comes commitment, as the various guests talk about the uses and benefits of the products the company sells that they already own, and consistency, as they purchase more to prove their commitment. When the buying begins, the doubters jump in, which is social proof in action. Rarely does anyone ever leave a home sales party without making at least a small purchase, often of something they'd never go to a store and buy. And it all starts with liking the hostess.

AUTHORITY

Perhaps the strongest of all the weapons of influence is authority. Humans have a deep-seated sense of duty to authority. We respond with obedience to people whom we view in positions of authority, such as doctors, police officers, military officers, judges, teachers, and even simply very well-dressed businesspeople. This is why so many advertisements for medical and health-related products feature doctors or, indirectly, feature a "patient" who says, "I talked with my doctor, and he told me . . ." We also view institutions such as the government, universities, and major publications as having authority. In our business, for example, the IRS is clearly a strong authority figure, although more from a perspective of fear than anything else. But we have to deal with that with our clients every day. One of the ways we are able to establish our own authority is by quoting the *Wall Street Journal*, which is a respected authority in business and finance, when that paper called us "far and

> "I seek opportunity—not security . . . I want to take the calculated risk; to dream and to build, to fail and to succeed . . . I prefer the challenges of life to the guaranteed existence; the thrill of fulfillment to the stale calm of utopia . . . It is my heritage to stand erect, proud, and unafraid; to think and act for myself, enjoy the benefit of my creations, and to face the world boldly and say, this I have done."
> —Dean Alfange

away, the most successful tax resolution company." Strong salespeople know how to establish themselves as authorities through their appearance, as well as verbal and nonverbal cues.

SCARCITY

Opportunities seem more valuable to us when their availability is limited. Also, many people enjoy the prestige of having things that aren't common—collector's items, limited editions, and so on. Some will even be motivated to buy an item they don't particularly want just because of scarcity. In sales and marketing, we use this with techniques such as limited quantities (only five to a customer; when they're gone, they're gone) and deadlines (offer ends Friday). Adding the element of scarcity can be very persuasive, but you must make it believable.

Providing Your Sales Team with Support

Many organizations that deal in technology make the mistake of hiring technicians—such as computer programmers, engineers, etc.—as salespeople because their sales force needs the technical knowledge when talking to customers. The problem is that people who are good technicians aren't likely to be good salespeople. They may understand the technical side of the product, but they often can't translate those features into benefits for the customer, and they may not even like dealing with people. Your results will be better if you hire salespeople to sell, and then support them with training and assistance from your technical team, up to and including the idea of sending a technician on sales calls with a salesperson. Or use assessment tools to identify candidates for your sales positions who will be strong sales performers and also have the necessary technical skills or at least the ability to understand the technical side of your products or services.

I Hate Selling

Actually, I don't mind selling because I've learned how to do it, but it's not my natural role in a business, and it's not what I prefer doing. When I first started testing the model for JK Harris & Company, I was the only salesperson because I couldn't afford to hire someone. But my natural personality type isn't a good fit for a strong salesperson.

The four basic personality temperaments are artisan, guardian, idealist, and rational, and then under each of those temperaments are four types. I am an idealist-healer as defined in the personality typology developed by Dr. David Keirsey in his classic 1998 book, *Please Understand Me II*. Idealist-healers are agreeable and cooperative at work and keenly aware of people and their feelings. They relate well with most others; however, they're introverted and very reserved. Consequently, they're not a good match for a sales position. Understanding these basic personality temperaments and types will help you understand why you and others excel at some things and don't at others.

> *"Success isn't a result of spontaneous combustion. You must set yourself on fire."*
> —Arnold H. Glasgow

My point in this is twofold. First, as a business owner, you'll often find yourself doing things you don't really enjoy because they have to be done, and there's no one else available. Suck it up, and get it done. Second, if you're not a natural salesperson, you need to get someone—or more than one, depending on the size of your business—on your team who is.

Invest in Your Top Performers

The tendency of most companies is to invest most of their development resources in the underperformers, the salespeople who are struggling. They tend to pay far less attention to the top or even the midranking performers.

But consider the flaws in that approach: If you're a top performer bringing in the revenue, how does it make you feel to see all that attention being focused on the people who can't get the job done? And if you're a sales manager or company owner, does it make sense to spend a lot of time and effort trying to improve a marginal salesperson—or would it be smarter to invest that time and effort helping a top performer become even better? By focusing a significant portion of your development efforts on your top and midrange performers, you'll improve your overall sales performance, and you'll probably drag some of the ones in the bottom ranks up to the middle.

Your top performers are definitely motivated by money, but they also demand recognition. It's an ego issue. They want to know that they are seen as top performers.

At any given moment, almost half the top sales performers are looking for another job where they will be better rewarded and recognized. If you want to keep your superstars, you need to figure out what motivates them (a whole person assessment will tell you that), and reward them appropriately.

With that said, let's be honest about this: Superstars aren't always easy to manage. Your top sales performers are eagles—strong, independent, and smart. You never see eagles flying in formation. But the more eagles you have, the better, because eagles try harder when they're surrounded by other eagles. They're competitive. They want to fly the highest, and they look at the other eagles and think, "If they can do it, I can do it better."

> "A lot of people have ideas, but there are few who decide to do something about them now. Not tomorrow. Not next week. But today. The true entrepreneur is a doer, not a dreamer."
> —Nolan Bushnell

Managing eagles is a challenge, which is why you need strong sales managers as well as top-notch salespeople.

There's Selling—Then There's Sales Management

There's a huge difference between a good salesperson and a good sales manager. In fact, the biggest problem in sales is not the salespeople, it's the sales managers.

It's very common for a business to promote its top salesperson to sales manager, but that's a perfect recipe for failure. The parameters for success in the two jobs are 180 degrees apart.

A great sales manager is a strong mentor, a coach, someone who enjoys spending time with salespeople, helping them develop and hone their skills. This isn't the way a sales superstar wants to spend his time—your best salespeople want to be out there *selling*, not managing other salespeople.

Your top salesperson will also probably be your worst sales teacher. Top salespeople don't know how to explain what they do; so much of it is intuitive, and they don't really understand it themselves. If they're asked to teach, they'll just say, "Watch me." But that doesn't work, because the people being trained need to be able to understand the whys behind the whats. I've tried to get our top sales performers to share their methods with the rest of our team, and they can't. It's not because they don't want to (although it's likely that many of them just don't want to be bothered); it really is because they simply don't know how to transfer that information.

Here's the bottom line on promoting your top salespeople to management: They'll be miserable, the people they're managing won't get the attention they deserve, and your overall performance will suffer. So don't do it. Reward those top salespeople in ways other than moving them into management—which really isn't a reward for them.

So where do the best sales managers come from? In our organization, they come from the ranks of the sales consultants who are above average but not at the top. These are people who know how to do the sales function, but their true passion is in managing and developing people. Their pure sales ability is at or slightly above average but not excellent. Where they excel is in coaching and mentoring. They like being out on the road with their salespeople. They're also good at numbers; they can analyze reports, understand results, and spot trends.

Our service is complex, and our sales consultants need a tremendous amount of technical knowledge to effectively sell it. This is why we never bring in an outsider as a sales manager; all our sales managers are promoted from within. A sales manager in any industry has to know what it's really like out there. We can identify people with management potential from the whole person assessment we do as part of our hiring process. And many of them tell us upfront: They're applying for a sales position, but their goal is to move into management. We work with those people to develop a career path that will meet both their needs and the company's. A lot of people who want to move into sales management will take a job with a company in sales hoping to progress into management. If you have salespeople with this mind-set who joined your team expecting to be promoted, yet you're going outside to hire managers and not moving these people up, they'll leave—and your company will suffer a loss.

We deliberately don't hire a lot of sales consultants who would rather be managers. Probably 20 percent or less of our sales consultants have management potential, and that gives us a sufficient pool of potential sales managers while most of our sales consultants are happy where they are. We want those sales consultants focusing on making sales, not getting promoted.

Managing and Motivating Your Sales Team

The first step in building a powerhouse of a sales team is to make sure you have the right people, and you do that through whole person assessments. If you hire salespeople with the right personality and give them sufficient training, managing them will be easy.

When it comes to motivating your sales team—well, you can't. You can't motivate anyone else, they have to motivate themselves. The late Bill Brooks, who I have mentioned before and from whom I learned a great deal about sales and sales management, said it this way in his book *The New Science of Selling and Persuasion*: "Motivation is only a portion of the sales success formula. Properly applied product knowledge, selling skills, strong interpersonal skills, and enjoying the success sales can bring are just as important and lead to sustained motivation." If you manage your sales team well, they'll motivate themselves.

Create a Culture of Constant Training

Training your sales team is critical, and you can't just do it once and assume it's done. Ongoing training and mentorship are two critical elements of sales management. After their initial training, which is grueling, our sales consultants have a variety of ongoing training opportunities throughout the year. In addition, our senior consultants have the opportunity to volunteer to mentor the new consultants. It's extra work, of course, so we compensate them by paying them an override on the sales plus a bonus based on the overall performance of the individuals they mentor. The mentoring program lets us avoid hiring full-time trainers to stay on the road with our new consultants, and the senior consultants learn as much from the experience as do the junior consultants.

We don't just pay lip service to the idea of training—we live it. It doesn't come cheap, but it's worth every penny.

Inspect What You Expect

The primary rule of sales management is to inspect what you expect. This is a good rule to apply to managing anyone in any position. Certainly give people the space they need to do their jobs, but make your expectations clear, and then make sure those expectations are met. People are more likely to do what you expect if they know you're going to come back and inspect it.

> *"You get out in front—you stay out in front."*
> —A. J. Foyt

I check our sales reports on a daily basis. As the CEO, I don't look at the numbers with the kind of attention to detail that our executive vice president of sales and marketing does. He's looking at what the regional managers do every day, and the regional managers are looking at what the sales

A Telephone Sales Team Can Do More than Telephone Sales

We used to have a call center that housed about 80 appointment-setters and another 15 telephone sales reps. We have phased out the call center as a physical place and now have those people working from their homes (the story of how the call center evolved is part of Strategy 7). The telephone sales reps handle calls from people who owe less than a certain amount of back taxes and meet other parameters that indicate their situation can be handled without a face-to-face meeting with a sales consultant.

Moving the telephone sales reps to their homes also allowed us to strategically position them around the country so they can serve as a backup to the sales consultants in the field, particularly in densely populated metropolitan areas, such as New York. When an office gets overloaded, we can pull a telephone sales rep to help cover the office temporarily. And when we have an opening for a sales consultant, our telephone sales reps who are interested in getting out into the field permanently get the first shot at the position, and when they do that, they're able to hit the ground running.

flashpoint

consultants who report to them do every day. I look at the company's overall performance, and I let the people who are responsible for the details do their jobs.

Show Them the Money

Salespeople are motivated by money.

Yes, they're also motivated by other things, such as recognition, power, and achievement, but the primary motivator of a good salesperson is money. Nonsalespeople are often more motivated by nonmonetary issues, such as respect, appreciation, opportunities for advancement, and the satisfaction of the work itself. But the people with true sales personalities, the salespeople who will perform in the top 10 percent, are motivated by money. You can give all the awards and recognition you want, but if you aren't writing a check along with it, they're not going to be motivated.

So how do you deliver that money? The best sales compensation is a combination of salary plus incentive. It took me many years to reach this conclusion and see it work, because I used to be a firm proponent of commission-only. But with a salary plus incentive plan, we get better quality sales and have fewer consumer complaints than we did with the commission-only plan.

> "Regardless of how you feel inside, always try to look like a winner. Even if you're behind, a sustained look of control and confidence can give you a mental edge that results in victory."
> —Arthur Ashe

This was actually one of the good things that came out of the attorney general (AG) investigations. When the investigations began, we were paying our salespeople a modest draw against commission only, plus expenses. It took the average consultant about six months to build enough sales to generate a commission pipeline that exceeded the draw, but once they reached that point, they were making a more-than-comfortable income.

The AGs felt that the commission-only compensation plan provided too much temptation for our sales consultants to engage in high-pressure sales tactics and perhaps cut corners when it came to making sure our clients really understood what they were contracting for. They insisted that we change to a salary plus incentive plan. I held out for a year until they said they wouldn't settle unless we agreed to change the sales compensation.

Figuring out how to put together a plan that would be fair, provide sufficient sales incentive, and satisfy the AGs was a challenge, but we did it. And in the first three months after we made the change, we lost half of our sales force. And before a year was over, we replaced most of the other half because they couldn't function under the new compensation program.

We had done an excellent job of recruiting and hiring top sales producers, but it was a team of people who had a personality type that typically wants to work on a commission-only basis. Our new compensation program measured performance in terms of bottom-line sales but also in a variety of other ways. In terms of benefit to the company and the clients, it was ten times better than the old incentive plan. We have a much better sales force today than we did before.

Regardless of how you structure your sales compensation, if your sales force is performing, they should be some of the top-paid people in your organization. Hire the very best people you can afford. Remember, if you pay peanuts, you'll get monkeys.

What Is Each Sale Really Worth?

Some sales are easier than others. Sometimes a salesperson has to use every ounce of skill he has to close a deal; sometimes he just gets lucky and the sale goes through smoother than a training script. We decided to take that into consideration as we formulated our new compensation plan. We also decided to consider how many appointments consultants had to keep to reach their total sales, the closing ratio, the client retention rate, as well as some additional factors that we hadn't been calculating before. We began measuring performance by what we call the average weighted value of each transaction instead of the bottom-line total sales. It was a huge eye-opener.

We had a consultant we thought was a superstar. Working commission-only out of our Miami office, she made more than $240,000 in commissions selling our services in 2006. Looking strictly at her sales volume, she was our number-one sales consultant. But we implemented the new plan, and she left three days later. When we started looking closely at the numbers beneath her numbers, we realized why. Our Miami office had so much traffic coming through it that she was able to cherry-pick the good clients and essentially run the others out the door. In terms of dollars alone, she was our top producer. But when we measured her performance under the new standards, she ranked in the 60th percentile.

Our marketing and sales system works this way: We run direct response ads, and use a variety of other marketing methods to get prospective clients to either call us on the phone or go to our website. Our appointment agents gather some preliminary information on the phone and schedule a time for the prospective client to come into one of our offices to meet with a sales consultant. At that session, the sales consultant reviews the client's situation and puts together a plan for dealing with it. If the client accepts the plan, the sale is made.

Under our commission-only plan, we held consultants responsible for being in the office when they had an appointment, but if the prospect didn't show up, we didn't charge that against their closing percentage. We figured, how could a consultant sell something to somebody who didn't show up? And because they were being paid on their total sales, we thought it didn't really matter. We did, however, expect them to see every client who did show up and to offer those clients a solution, even if the solution wasn't lucrative for us.

Most of our consultants worked the way we expected them to, even when they knew, for example, that a client didn't owe enough in back taxes to make it worth their while to sign on with us and pay our fees. But there were a few—like the consultant in Miami we thought was doing so great—who figured out how to game our system. They would get on the phone the night before and call everyone who had appointments scheduled for the next day. They'd review the preliminary information from the appointment center, ask a few questions, and if the prospect's situation didn't sound like a good opportunity for a sale, they'd give the client some general advice on how to handle the situation themselves and cancel the appointment. Because we didn't know about the phone call, that prospect went into our system as a no-show. Those consultants had great closing ratios and total sales numbers because they weren't seeing the challenging clients.

But the company was still making the investment to put prospects in front of those consultants. It costs us $150 in advertising to put a prospective client in front of our sales consultants. But when prospects don't keep their appointments—whether they just decide not to or a consultant calls them ahead of time and tells them not to show up—that increases the real cost of the ones that are seen. If a few consultants are chasing off prospects that they have prejudged as not sufficiently lucrative, that hurts the company *and* the other consultants who are working honestly and according to our terms.

When you operate with a commission-only compensation plan, it's natural to think that your highest-paid salespeople are your best salespeople. When we changed to a salary plus incentive plan, we realized that's not always true. In fact, we determined that our consultants with the highest dollar volume in sales were actually *not* our best consultants because they were focused on their own bottom line over giving our prospective clients the attention they deserve.

A well-crafted salary plus incentive plan levels the playing field for your sales team. Nobody is at an advantage or disadvantage because of their territory—they all have the same opportunities to excel in this system.

Sell First, Last, and Always

What I learned from the story of Oracle is a key reason why JK Harris & Company is the largest tax representation firm in the country. When I first launched the business, I was focusing on building the best possible service on the back end, and my plan was to grow the business slowly. Then I realized that my plan was the fast track to obscurity at best and failure at worst, so about a year into it, I shifted gears.

In the early 1990s, the tax representation industry was under-served and fragmented. Few practitioners were specializing in it, and no one was doing any serious marketing. For most people, a problem with the IRS meant you could spend tens of thousands of dollars on accountants and attorneys or—if you couldn't afford that—take your chances dealing directly with the IRS yourself. There was a clear need in the marketplace for tax representation that was both effective and affordable for individuals and small businesses.

I'd like to be able to say that I was the only person with the vision to recognize that, but I wasn't. In fact, I hadn't thought about tax representation as a business until I had a client with my CPA practice who needed major help with an IRS debt. A few other entrepreneurs had figured out the potential and were starting their own tax representation firms. But the industry was in its infancy with no clear leader.

I made two critical decisions: One, I decided that JK Harris & Company was going to be the leader in the tax representation industry. Two, I decided that if I was going to end up on top, just like Oracle did in the database industry, I'd better do what Larry Ellison did. I had to grow the company and its brand identity as fast as I could. I had to make sure that by the time anybody else woke up and realized this industry was here, it was too late for them—they wouldn't be able to compete with me. And that meant pouring coals on the sales and marketing fire I had built and getting my offices opened as fast as possible.

Unlike Oracle, we did *not* have a flawed product. The service we provided was in accordance with the best professional practices. But even so, there was room for improvement. For example, as I've said previously, we were getting the work done, but we weren't always responding to our clients the way they wanted. We weren't returning calls as quickly as some clients expected. We weren't communicating as effectively as we could have. That was the nature of virtually all the complaints we got in those days. Certainly fixing that was a high priority for me, but sales and marketing were even higher priorities. I knew that I would only be able to stake my position as the industry leader with the successful implementation of an effective sales and marketing plan, so that's what I did.

The Bottom Line

Understand the total cost of your sales—and what it costs you when you don't make them. That's what you're losing when you don't make the sale. In our case, we know exactly how much it costs us to get a prospective client in front of one of our sales consultants, and we know what we lose when the sale doesn't close. This is a critical element of sales management as well as maintaining overall profitability.

My original plan called for opening four new offices a month. At the end of the first year, I tripled that and was opening 12 new offices every month. Along with that, I was establishing sales territories, hiring and training both sales and support staff, and getting people into the field to do the work. At the end of our third year, we had built out our entire sales network two years ahead of the original schedule.

I take extraordinary pride in our sales team. They are true professionals, committed as much to the success of the company as they are to their own. But I also know that if the company stops supporting them, compensating them, and providing the opportunities they seek, they'll be out the door. And I think that's fair.

—— KEY LESSONS ——

✳ *No product or service is so good that it sells itself.* No matter how good or how essential a product is, it needs to be supported by strong sales and marketing efforts to be successful.

✳ *With the right sales and marketing efforts, mediocre (and worse) products can be successful.* That's because products don't sell themselves, they're sold by people.

✳ *Create a culture in your organization that encourages your sales and marketing teams to work together.* Make communication and interaction between these two groups mandatory, and recognize and respect their mutual contributions.

✳ *Anyone can—and should—learn basic selling skills,* but only people with a natural sales temperament will develop into sales superstars.

✳ *The most valuable selling skill you can develop is the power of persuasion.* To do this, you need to understand why people buy what they buy and how they make their buying decisions. Then you can use various persuasive techniques to help them reach a decision that is also compatible with your goals.

* *Persuasion and manipulation are two very different things.* Persuasion influences someone to make a decision on his own. Manipulation uses control and trickery to get someone to do what you want them to do, even though they're not truly committed to the action.

* *The five key ways to use persuasion in the sales process are reciprocation, commitment and consistency, social proof, liking, authority, and scarcity.* Reciprocation involves doing something for someone that creates an obligation for them to do something (usually make a purchase) for you. Commitment and consistency is based on the fact that once people make a commitment, they'll behave in ways that are consistent with that commitment. So if they make the commitment that they like and want or need your product, consistent behavior would be to make the purchase. The concept of social proof means that people look to others for guidance when they aren't sure what to do, so if others are buying from you, they will also. Like builds on the sense of obligation people feel to purchase from people they like, which is why the home party sales approach can be so successful. Human beings have a natural tendency to respond with obedience to authority, and when an authority—either a salesperson who has established himself as such or another entity that's a recognized authority—suggests a purchase, chances are high that it will happen. Finally, scarcity creates the sense that something is more valuable because it's not widely and readily available, and many people are driven by a need to have what others can't.

* *Give your salespeople the technical support they need,* but don't make the mistake of putting a technical person without a strong sales personality into a sales position.

🔆 *Invest in your top performers.* Recognize and reward them, stroke their egos—and they'll go to great lengths to outdo themselves. Don't make the mistake of thinking they don't need your attention because they're doing so well. If they start to feel neglected and unappreciated, they'll start looking for another opportunity, and you'll lose them.

🔆 *Don't spend too much time on the bottom performers.* Certainly if you can help them improve, you should—but not at the expense of the people who are doing a good job. Provide sufficient training and coaching, and if they can't pull themselves out of the bottom 20 percent, let them go.

🔆 *Recognize the difference between good salespeople and strong sales managers.* Your top salespeople will rarely be good sales managers, so don't promote them and set them up to fail. Good sales managers are typically above-average salespeople, but not superstars, who also enjoy mentoring and coaching, as well as administration.

🔆 *Ongoing training is essential.* Salespeople need regular product knowledge education as well as sales skills training. It also helps to periodically bring them together as a group so they can be energized from each other.

🔆 *Make your expectations clear and follow up to make sure your expectations are being met.* People need to know you're paying attention.

🔆 *If you have a telephone sales team, use them as a backup to your field team.* When you have an opening in the field, give the telephone sales team the first crack at it. Not all of them will want to go out in the field, but the ones that do can hit the ground running because they already know your operation.

🔆 *Develop a sales compensation plan that provides financial incentives for outstanding performance but is also structured to prevent high-pressure sales and reward salespeople for taking an appropriate amount of time with less-lucrative customers.* Create a level playing field so there's no advantage or disadvantage based on territory.

* *Know what each sale costs you to close* and what it's worth in terms of revenue and profits.

* *Support your sales team* with a good product, training, marketing, compensation, and recognition.

Respect the Competition

When I first launched JK Harris & Company, I was focused on carrying out my plan, staying on track with my growth strategy, and making sure I had enough cash to open the next offices on my list and hire the necessary people to staff those offices and serve the clients. At the time, there was virtually no competition—just a few CPAs, attorneys, and retired IRS employees who were enrolled agents offering tax resolution services. Most of the CPAs and attorneys were offering tax resolution as part of an overall service package, and most of the enrolled agents who had retired from the IRS just wanted enough work to keep busy and supplement their pensions. I didn't see any reason to pay much attention to them. I knew they were there, but they weren't getting in my way, so I ignored them. Even better for me, they were clueless about what I was doing. They weren't thinking like entrepreneurs. I used that to my advantage and got so far out in front of them that by the time they realized it, there was absolutely no way they could catch up.

Today, JK Harris & Company is still far and away the nation's largest tax resolution firm. We're ten times the size of our nearest competitor. But that doesn't mean I can ignore the competition. I subscribe to the philosophy of Sun Tzu, a Chinese general and military strategist from about 400 B.C., who was quoted by the Michael Corleone character in *The Godfather*: "Keep your friends close, and your enemies closer."

Engage in Competitive Camaraderie

Of course, your competitors aren't actually your enemies. Think about all the professional associations for various industries. One key thing associations do is allow competitors to stay close, to share information, and to work together for their own benefit as well as the improvement of the industry. When I bought my asphalt paving company, one of the first things the guy I bought it from did was take me to a meeting of the local asphalt pavers association. The total association consisted of maybe five or six contractors, and their only "official" activity was meeting for dinner once a month. But it was through those meetings that I learned so much of what I needed to know to operate my business and survive in the particular political environment of the time. Yes, every person at those meetings was a competitor, but we also had a "we're in this together" camaraderie that worked.

Today, I know who my competitors are. I pay attention to their marketing. My ad agency tracks where they are placing their ads and how much they're spending, and provides me with regular reports. I look at their ad content. I know what they're offering and what emotional strings they're pulling. I know what geographic areas they serve and how they sell and deliver their services. And my smart competitors know all that about me.

A while back I invited the owners of all the tax resolution services that I consider to be competition (by that I mean companies that are marketing and trying to grow—not the semi-retired enrolled agent or CPA who's offering this service as either a part-time job or as part of a different type of professional practice) to come to Charleston for an industry retreat. They were responsible for their own transportation, but I paid for everything else. We had a wonderful three days of open discussion about our business. I found out that we were pretty much all facing the same challenges, and we had some great exchanges of ideas on ways to deal with those issues. I learned things about them that are important for me to know. I'm sure they learned things about me that they'll be able to use to their advantage.

We agreed that the adage "a rising tide lifts all boats" can be applied to our industry in the context of creating an operating environment that includes self-regulation, a code of ethics and conduct, and consumer protection standards. Because of that, we intend to cooperate in advancing the image and reputation of our industry. I'm sure we'll be meeting again. In the meantime, of course, we're back on our own turfs, competing with as much energy and resources as we can muster.

Your Competition Can Make You Better

When a competitor is beating you, do the best you can to figure out why, and don't use that as an excuse to accept defeat. Once you understand what they're doing right, take a look at what you're doing wrong and fix it. Even if you're not doing anything wrong, look for what you can do to improve.

Whether or not a competitor is ahead of you, study them for ideas. If they're smart enough (or dumb enough) to get in the same business you're in, they're probably smart enough to have come up with some new strategies in product, service, and marketing. Just keep in mind that if you're inspired by what they're doing and want to see how taking a similar approach might work for you, take care that you don't violate any intellectual property rights, such as copyrights or patents. Also, don't assume that everything they're doing works—test and measure to find out for sure.

Then There's the Rockefeller Approach

Convinced that the real profit in oil was in refining, not drilling, John D. Rockefeller bought his first refinery in 1863. The Civil War was under way and the demand for kerosene and other refined oil products was growing, but there were too many refineries, and competition was driving prices down. Rockefeller's strategy for dealing with competition was to buy them out or drive them out. He bought them if he could, and if they wouldn't sell, he drove them out of business using cutthroat competition and railroad rebates, which were special low fares railroads charged their favored customers. His strategy made him a robber baron in the eyes of his competitors, as well as the journalists and politicians of the time. He was a brilliant but ruthless entrepreneur and became one of the most hated men in America.

> *"Never underestimate the other guy."*
> —Jack Welch

I believe there are times when cutthroat competition is justified, and I will tell you about one such circumstance later on. But most of the time, your company can be strong and profitable while you sleep well at night if you engage in healthy, fair competition.

Tracking the Competition

It really is easy to find out what your competition is up to. You don't have to tap their phone lines or dig through their garbage— you don't even have to invite them to visit you, as I did. They're not keeping what they're doing a secret because they want their customers to know about it. So keep an eye on the articles that mention them in trade journals, newspapers, and magazines. Review their websites periodically. Do regular internet searches on them so you know what's being said on other websites. If possible and practical, "secret shop" them regularly to observe firsthand how they function in a sales situation.

When you've identified your competitors, set up intelligence files on each of them. In addition, you might want to create a comparison chart so that you have an at-a-glance snapshot of every player in your market. Make sure that your sales and customer service teams have access to this information so they are prepared to respond to any comments your customers or prospective customers might make about one of your competitors.

When you see your competition doing something right, figure out how you can use the same technique. When you see them doing something wrong, highlight the advantage you offer in your marketing messages. For example, in our advertisements, we emphasize the fact that we meet with our clients personally, face-to-face, at one of our hundreds of locations nationwide. We don't say "our competition will only talk to you on the phone"—we don't have to. Our customers can figure that out on their own.

The Disadvantage of Being the Industry Leader

As I've mentioned, our nearest competitor does about one-tenth of the volume we do. None of the other tax resolution firms uses the same business model that we do. We have hundreds of offices across the country, and we sell face-to-face. They typically have one main office and sell over the phone. In large part because of that in-person contact, our closing rate is four to five times higher than their closing rate.

But there's a disadvantage of being the leader, especially in a relatively new, highly fragmented, and largely unregulated industry, and that is that we're not only the biggest in terms of employees, offices, and revenue, we're also the biggest target when it comes to investigations and litigation. There's just no point in filing a class action suit against a firm doing a couple of million dollars a year in business, because they don't have enough assets to make it worthwhile, even if the plaintiffs win. We do.

When we negotiated settlements with the group of 18 attorneys general (AGs), we agreed to remove certain phrases from our advertising. We didn't feel there was anything wrong with the phrases we were using, but the AGs did, and we decided it was best to reach an agreement rather than take the issue to court. So we used to be able to talk about settling your IRS debt for "pennies on the dollar"—something that can be done for taxpayers who qualify using the IRS's offer in compromise program. We agreed to stop using that phrase and a few others, but our competitors can go out there and claim to settle an IRS debt for pennies on the dollar all day long, and the AGs leave them alone because they're not big enough to bother with.

I know for a fact that the words and phrases we've agreed not to use draw more response from prospective customers than what we're allowed to say, so when our competition uses those words, it puts us at a disadvantage. Average consumers don't have any idea that we're prohibited by the terms of our agreement with the AGs from using the same marketing messages that our competitors are still able to use. So when they hear the other firms promising to "settle your tax debt for pennies on the dollar" and showing client testimonials to that effect, but we aren't making such promises, they probably think that the other firms can actually do that for anyone, but we can't.

Our response to that disadvantage is to be smarter than our competition and to out-market them. Because of our size, we can spend more money marketing than they can. Our closest competitor spends about $400,000 a month on advertising. Our monthly ad budget is $1.2 million. That competitor spends its entire ad budget on national cable television ads. We'll spend the same amount on national cable, and on top of that, we'll spend another $800,000 on the internet, direct mail, radio, public relations, and other marketing avenues. In addition, we sell face-to-face. We have offices across the country that our clients can come to and talk to a sales consultant in person; our competitors don't.

> "In the book of life, the answers aren't in the back."
> —Charlie Brown

We became the nation's largest tax resolution firm because I set that as a goal when I started the company. We have stayed the nation's largest tax resolution firm because we know our business, and we do it well. So in our ads, we use testimonials that don't mention specific dollar amounts but stress the peace of mind we've delivered for our clients, and we stress our size and longevity. If we could use some of the words we've agreed not to use, we would definitely have an even larger market share than we do now. But we can't.

Is that fair? No. But it's the way the world is. I've learned to accept it and deal with it, because I can't change it. And even with the competitive disadvantage from the marketing perspective, we've stayed on top.

When the Competition Plays Dirty

I think fair competition is great. It creates a "may the best company win" situation and forces everyone to do their best. But you will have competitors who don't play fair. When that happens, you need to consider the situation, and take appropriate action.

The internet has made playing dirty easier than ever. Back in 2000, one of our competitors set up a couple of different websites using JK Harris in metatags, keywords, and source code so that if you searched for us, you got his site. And on his site, he had some very defamatory and false information about us. That was before Google was the primary search engine and internet marketing was still in its infancy, so it took us a while to even figure out what was going on. Today, with the search engines using the technology that they do, this probably wouldn't work because the search engines would figure it out. But back then, once we realized what he'd done, we knew we had to take action.

We obtained an injunction that forced him to temporarily take the sites down. He claimed First Amendment rights and was allowed to put the sites back up, but he was ordered to remove the metatags and source code. In the meantime, we launched the beginnings of our own search engine marketing strategy (we didn't know at the time that's what it was called) of actively putting positive information about our company on the internet.

The First Amendment does make it difficult to take action about websites that say negative things about you, but it doesn't protect people from publishing outright false statements. Still, policing the internet is a huge challenge for any company. We have several employees along with outside consultants on our team who are constantly monitoring what's being said about us on other websites, blogs, discussion boards, and so on, and making decisions about what to do about it. Unfortunately, some companies aren't satisfied with trying to tell the world how good they are; they feel like they have to slam the competition in a sneaky, unethical way.

Not All Speech Is Protected

The Lanham Trademark Act of 1946, which deals primarily with issues related to trademark infringement, trademark dilution, and false advertising, has a provision which allows a company to sue a competitor for unfair trade practices—which is essentially a nice term for "dirty tricks." We found this out when a New York attorney/CPA sued us and one of our competitors under the Lanham Act, alleging that our respective marketing and advertising practices were giving the tax resolution industry a bad name and costing him business.

We made an economic decision to settle the lawsuit rather than fight it. I don't believe he had a valid claim—or, as the lawyers would phrase it, the suit was without merit—but it would have cost us hundreds of thousands of dollars and who knows how much time to let the case work its way through the courts. But in the process of evaluating the situation and deciding how best to handle it, we

> *"The guy who takes a chance, who walks the line between the known and unknown, who is unafraid of failure, will succeed."*
> —Gordon Parks

learned that anyone can sue virtually anyone else for unfair trade practices and claim economic damages. This particular lawsuit provided us with some valuable education for dealing with competitors who try to play dirty, because we have used this act to our own benefit since then. Of course, as is the case with any lawsuit, filing the suit and winning it are two completely different things, but the Lanham Act offers some ammunition we didn't realize we had.

Don't Let It Slide

You have a right to protect your reputation and that of your company. When you become aware of anyone saying or writing things about you that aren't true and are designed to hurt your business, you should take immediate action. In many cases, a simple cease-and-desist letter will do the job. Send a firmly worded letter to the offending company outlining exactly what they're doing—whether it's information on a website, in their advertising, or something their reps are saying—and saying that you believe what they're doing constitutes unfair trade practices and if they don't stop you'll pursue all possible remedies, up to and including legal action. Send the letter via certified mail, return receipt requested, so you can prove that you sent it and that it was received. You can write this letter yourself; you don't need a lawyer to do it.

If the letter doesn't resolve the problem, it's time to take it up a notch and refer the matter to your attorney. Often a company that ignores your letter will respond to one from an attorney because they don't want to get involved in expensive litigation. If the attorney letter doesn't work, you need to evaluate the situation, and make a business decision about how far you want to take it.

The same approach applies to your intellectual property. If someone infringes on your trademarks, copyrights, patents, or other protected information, take immediate action. Failure to do so when you find out about it could negate your right to take action later. These days, most trademark and copyright infringement occurs on the internet, so monitor the web for unauthorized use of your name and marks. If the infringement is an honest mistake, a cease-and-desist letter will probably resolve the situation.

The World Wide Web Is Like the Wild, Wild West

For all the positive aspects of the internet—such as expanding your markets and leveling the playing field for small companies—the World Wide Web has its share of negatives.

One issue that can work both for you and against you is that the internet offers a 24/7, worldwide forum for your customers and competitors to talk about you. If they're saying nice things, wonderful. But chances are, at least some of the comments posted on various websites will be negative. And of those, some will be justified and some won't. You'll have competitors who will post negative information that contains just enough truth to make it impossible for you to do anything about. For example, someone could truthfully say that we've been raided by the IRS and investigated by a number of attorneys general—without telling the whole story and saying that we were never even *charged* with any wrong-doing, much less convicted. Any time anything negative happens to you, be prepared for your competitors to take it out of context and use it against you. That's why you need a crisis management plan in place before you need it, which I discussed in Strategy 4.

Another internet challenge is the issue of domain names. This was much easier to manage back when there were only four basic types of domain names (.com, .gov, .org, and .edu). There have been a significant number of court cases involving situations where someone has purchased and put up websites with names such as *companysucks.com* and *companynoservice.com*. Smart companies go ahead and purchase those domains so that nobody else can use them. Today, however, with a virtually limitless number of domain name extensions, competitors, detractors, and even simple opportunists can buy a domain name that's a version of your company name and put up a site that at worst defames you and at best just directs viewers elsewhere. It's impossible to buy every variation of your name, so you have to be diligent in monitoring what's out there and go after cases of trademark infringement as soon as you discover them.

Legislation and case law have not yet caught up with what's happening on the internet, and who knows if they ever will? The internet is a largely unregulated, anything-goes place. Your best bet is to understand it, accept it, and learn to work with it on its own terms.

The Nuisance Competitor

Sometimes competitors do things that are more annoying than damaging. We have had, for example, competitors open accounts with overnight courier services in our name, with the goal of having us pick up those expenses. We've also had competitors open offices in the same building where we're located and hang out in the lobby, waiting to snag our clients as they come in. You'd like to think that people with the wherewithal to open a business would be above such childish, petty games, but that's not always the case. My policy is to pay attention, respond as appropriate (in the above two situations, we refused to pay the courier bill and made sure our appointment-setters were very clear with instructions on how to find our offices), and never stoop to such an unprofessional level.

It's Not Illegal to Be Stupid

As you evaluate your competition, consider whether they're deliberately doing things that are against the law—such as defamation and trademark infringement—or whether they're just dumb, such as selling below cost without a logical strategy for doing that. You'll find it's much easier to deal with the criminals than the competitors who are stupid because you have legal recourse against the criminals.

In *How to Sell at Margins Higher than Your Competitors*, Lawrence L. Steinmetz and William T. Brooks write: "Whom would you rather compete against, a crook or an idiot? If you think about it, you'll no doubt decide in favor of a crook. Have you ever seen a crook sell below cost? . . . Have you ever seen an idiot sell below cost? Fundamentally, it is not the crook we fear in business, but rather it is the honest idiot. The people (or organizations) who don't know what they are doing are the ones who foul up the works."

> *"The bitterness of poor quality remains long after the sweetness of low price is forgotten."*
> —Unknown

Eventually, your stupid competitors will put themselves out of business. Until they do, let them have the customers who buy on price and you go after the customers who want quality and service. Your crooked competitors are a different story; with them, you need to take quick, decisive action that's appropriate to the situation.

When Employees Become Competitors

At JK Harris & Company, we do a lot of things to keep our turnover rate as low as possible, because turnover is expensive. But people will leave, and sometimes they leave to go to work for competing organizations. That's just the way things are. We do our best to protect our operation when that happens by having strong noncompete and nondisclosure agreements our employees sign. But it's one thing to lose a single individual to a competitor. It's altogether something else when your employees *become* competitors.

At one point, we had a group of key people leave to form a competing company. I didn't take it personally. It's what happens in business. But I also had no intention of sitting back, wishing them well, and doing nothing while our market share eroded.

There are plenty of people out there whose idea of starting a "new" business is to simply go do what everybody else is doing and take market share from the other players. They're not creating a new product or generating a new demand; they're just jumping into and diluting an existing market. All they're doing is dividing the pie into smaller slices.

What does that accomplish? It makes the competition vicious, and it drives down prices. That's capitalism and competition at work. And, at least for a while, it's great for the consumer. But eventually some of the companies will fail, and after they do, competition isn't quite so fierce.

Here's how the cycle goes: Let's say that a particular market worth about $5 million is being well-served by four players. Somebody who works for one of those players decides to start a competing company. Somebody else decides the industry looks attractive and decides to jump in as well. Now there are six players dividing up that $5 million. Maybe the market could have supported five players, but not six. So at least one of those six isn't going to make it. There might also be a player or two that's particularly strong and savvy, and who may be able to take advantage of the turmoil in the market and capture even more market share than they had previously.

How do you make sure you're one of the survivors? You do it by knowing your industry and your business better than the other players, by being more aggressive, and by being more competitive. And if being more competitive means temporarily driving the prices down to an unsustainable level, you have to evaluate whether or not you have enough capital to survive the price war and be one of the ones that remains standing when the dust settles.

When the guys broke off from us to form their own competing tax resolution company, they opened up in maybe 12 or 14 markets—and in some of those markets, they even set up their offices in the same buildings, the same executive suites, we were in. They weren't doing anything different. They weren't creating new business. The number of potential clients wasn't increasing or decreasing based on anything they were doing. There's nothing a tax resolution firm can do to affect the size of the market.

As it happened, I had a slight edge in this situation because I knew how much money they had. Somebody had slipped up and told me. And because they were doing exactly what we did, I knew what it was going to cost them to get up and running and to operate. I figured they had enough cash to survive for six months, and if I helped them along by giving them some serious price competition, I could cut that to four months.

I knew that we had the financial strength to survive a short-term period of price cuts in the markets where this new company was competing against us. So that's what we did. And the strategy worked.

Sometimes you can play softball—but sometimes you have to play hardball.

Sleep with One Eye Open

Never take your eyes off the competition. Do your best to stay ahead of them, to change your strategy and prevent them from copying you, to stretch and reach so they can't catch you. Do your best to win every round, but know that you won't always. Sometimes you'll just have to clean up the mess after the fact and move on. Just like you can take market share away from someone else, someone can do it to you as well. Be vigilant. Know who your competitors are—both old and new players. Remember that the closer you are to the top, the further you have to fall—and the bigger the crash you'll make if you hit the bottom.

If you're successful, you're going to have competition. If you're making money, somebody else is going to want a piece of your action. So be prepared for it. And never underestimate the competition.

———— KEY LESSONS ————

✷ *Don't ignore the competition.* Certainly your primary focus should be on your own business, but you must always keep track of your competitors. Pay attention to where they are, what they're offering, and how they're marketing. Study their ads. Periodically visit their websites. Read what's written about them in trade publications and other media. If possible, "secret shop" them to find out how they sell.

✷ *Let your competitors make you better.* To stay ahead of the competition, you have to be the best you can be. Let them push you toward that goal.

✳ *Being the industry leader—or at least being a large company—has its drawbacks.* The bigger you are, the bigger target you become. Regulators, consumer advocates, and attorneys don't bother going after the little guys because they have little to gain even if they win.

✳ *Know what to do if the competition doesn't play fair.* If they're doing something that's against the law, take appropriate action. Often a cease-and-desist letter will resolve the situation. If it doesn't, consult an attorney.

✳ *Protect your reputation and your intellectual property.* Don't let any infringement slide or you'll lose your right to protect it in the future.

✳ *Develop solid noncompete, nondisclosure, and confidentiality agreements* for employees to protect your proprietary information should someone leave your company to go to work for a competitor or to start a competing company.

✳ *Fight fire with fire.* Always operate legally and ethically, but play hardball when you have to.

Prepare for Success

It's generally assumed that money is the result of and reason for business success. That may be true for some, but not everyone. To put money in perspective: It's a tool. Money is designed for one thing: to generate more money. That's all money is for.

Money in and of itself isn't a goal to me. Money is a byproduct of work, perseverance, and luck—being in the right place at the right time, recognizing the opportunities, and taking them. Money isn't the yardstick by which I measure success, but it can be an important tool in achieving success.

When you make money, you have to plow it back into your business to make sure the business is financially secure and can grow. If you take too much of it out, the company will suffer. When you have a financially secure, viable, profitable business that's growing, you can use the money it's making to accomplish a host of other things—you can develop innovative, new products and services; create jobs; make a positive impact on the economy; support whatever charity you like; and live the lifestyle of your choice.

Business leaders have a moral obligation to make their companies good corporate citizens but that will be difficult if the company isn't in good shape. Former General Electric chairman and CEO Jack Welch says that only healthy, winning companies have the resources to be socially responsible. In *Jack: Straight from the Gut*, he writes: "Only a healthy enterprise can improve and enrich the lives of people and their communities. When a company is strong, it not only pays taxes that provide for important services. It also builds world-class facilities that meet or exceed safety and environmental standards. Strong companies reinvest in their people and their facilities. Healthy companies provide good and secure jobs that give their employees time, the spirit, and the resources to give back to their communities a thousand-fold."

The way to become one of those companies is to be preparing for it from day one. When you're prepared for success, you can manage it and capitalize on it. You can build a business that will last.

If you're are not prepared for success, you may find it unmanageable and overwhelming. If you're lucky, you'll simply stumble and fall. If you're not, you'll crash and burn.

Solomon Software is a classic example of the need to be prepared for success. The company, which was founded in 1980 as TLB Inc., was doing well designing accounting software products. It was a small company with just a few employees that was profitable and growing steadily. Then, in 1985, their Solomon III product won the popular *PC Magazine*/Price Waterhouse "Editors' Choice" award. The company wasn't prepared for the impact that would have. You'd think such an award would be a good thing for a software company, and in the long run it was—but in the short term, it almost buried them because they weren't prepared to handle the success that came with the industry recognition. This small, manageable company was exploding—it had not just hit the flashpoint, it had gone beyond it. It was chaos for several years until the company's leaders managed to get the growth under control. Because they were able to do that, the company continued to grow and was eventually acquired by Microsoft.

One of Solomon Software's founders, Gary Harpst, went on to create a consulting firm and is the author of *Six Disciplines for Excellence* and *Six Disciplines: Execution Revolution*. He says, "Knowing how to plan and execute, while overcoming today's inevitable surprises, is the most foundational capability any successful organization can learn."

When you're putting together your business plan, it's easy to be optimistic in your forecasts. It's not quite so easy, but still doable, to discuss what could go wrong and what your contingency plans are.

But the real question is: When you put your plan into action and everything works, will you be prepared for your success? Let's discuss some of the key issues you need to consider so you're absolutely ready for success when it happens.

It Takes Cash to Grow

A general rule is that the faster you grow, the more cash you're going to need to fund that growth. And growth financing is every bit as hard—if not harder—to get than startup funding. It's critical that you do regular cash-flow projections so you know how much credit you're going to need well in advance of the time you have to start writing checks. It's equally important that you have excellent relationships with your funding sources, as well as more than one source of capital.

Stay close to your lenders. Let them know what's going on— and always tell them the truth. I make it a practice to be totally

flashpoint

Great Expectations

Zig Ziglar says that you can achieve success by expecting success. He writes, "When you plan and prepare carefully, you can legitimately expect to have success in your efforts. When you recognize and develop the winning qualities that you were born with, the winner you were born to be emerges. . . . Also understand that the path from where you are to where you want to be is not always smooth and straight. The reason for the twists and bumps is simple, and it has nothing to do with you. It has more to do with the fact that not everyone is as interested in your success as you are. Some people may accidentally hinder your efforts; others who are in competition with you and have little or no integrity may try to sabotage your efforts. Keep in mind, though, that when you hit those roadblocks your character, commitment, and attitude are the determining factors in your success."

candid with my bankers. If something is happening that's going to affect us financially—good or bad—I want my bankers to hear it from me first. And my lenders reciprocate.

The old saying that it's easier to borrow money when you don't need it is true—and in today's financial climate, it's harder than ever to predict credit availability. You have to stay on top of your cash and financial needs so that you have plenty of room to maneuver when it's time to borrow. Don't get so wrapped up in growing your company that you forget to do what's necessary to fund that growth.

Is Growth Your Goal?

Take some time before you answer that question. Growth has been at least part of the goal of every business I've been involved with, whether it was as an owner, investor, or employee. I never wanted a small company; whatever I was involved in, whether it was as an

158

owner or employee, I wanted to grow it. But I've learned that growth for growth's sake isn't always the best strategy—and there may be situations where you can actually be more profitable if you're smaller. We've seen that many banks were more profitable when they were smaller, so why would we want them to grow? Who says your business has to grow? Is growth, particularly rapid growth, what you really want?

If you're in a young industry without a clear leader, then the answer to that last question is yes, because the well-managed,

Do You Want to Be a Rock Star?

There's a curious dynamic that occurs when a company grows to a certain number of employees, and the founder is still running the show. When you're small and you're working shoulder to shoulder with your employees, they see you as a regular person, someone they know and can identify with. But there comes a point when you become like a celebrity to your employees. Until JK Harris, I had not had a company big enough for this to happen, but I saw it at Wikoff. To say that the employees there worshiped Fred Wikoff is an exaggeration, but they definitely put him on a pedestal. I've also recognized the dynamic in other companies that are closely identified with their founders.

When I realized it was happening to me, I was very uncomfortable. But you really can't stop it. Even though I've always been committed to growth, I never thought I would have a company so big that I would have employees whose names I don't know, but that's the way it is now. And to them, I am something of a celebrity, at least in our little world. I keep myself grounded by remembering that underneath the image they admire, I'm still me. I appreciate the respect I receive, but I don't want adulation. I have a job to do, just like they do. I never forget that.

> *"Interestingly, koi, when put in a fish bowl, will only grow up to 3 inches. When this same fish is placed in a large tank, it will grow to about 9 inches long. In a pond koi can reach lengths of 18 inches. Amazingly, when placed in a lake, koi can grow to 3 feet long. The metaphor is obvious. You are limited by how you see the world."*
>
> —Vince Poscente

growing business is the one that will set the standards and survive the shakeout that will naturally occur as new players enter the market. That's why I grew JK Harris & Company to be as large as it is as fast as I did.

However, if you're in a more mature industry, you should do some careful analysis of your business, market, and goals before you decide on a growth plan. You may decide that your optimum profitability and performance levels will occur if you're not the biggest player on the field.

Never Stop Learning

Don't ever think you know enough, because you never will. Make it a point to learn something new every day—it's great exercise for your mind and will be a huge benefit to your company.

I do this primarily by reading. I have thousands of books in my library. I have bookshelves in my office and my home, in almost every room, and often taking up an entire wall of a room. I have read hundreds of biographies, and my bookshelves are also packed with the classics of Western literature, history books, and an abundance of contemporary business books. When I run out of shelf space, I build more. I also read electronic books—I have an Amazon Kindle that's a tremendous tool. But I like the printed page, I like to highlight things, mark pages with sticky-notes, and hold the book in my hands as I read. In fact, if I read an electronic book and really like it, I'll buy the printed version to have it in my library.

I also read newspapers, magazines, and study other information sources about my industry. I attend seminars and conferences. I invest in training. When I meet people who know more than I do, I pick their brains and learn everything I can from them.

If you stop learning, you'll stagnate, and so will your company. Develop a thirst for knowledge that will never be quenched.

Accounting Can Fool You

In business, a lot of accounting terms get tossed around—profit, net profit, gross profit, net worth, expenses, receivables, line of credit, etc. It's important to understand exactly what these terms mean, especially when they're applied to your own business or one you may want to invest in.

I don't like the day-to-day work of being an accountant, but my accounting background and the fact that I'm a CPA makes it easier for me when it comes to the financial side of business than it is for most entrepreneurs.

Consider this: At the end of our first five years in business, JK Harris & Company had a net worth of $6 million. That was what was left over after all our expenses were paid. What happened to that money? Did we spend it? No. Did we pay it out in bonuses or dividends? No. If we had spent it or paid it in bonuses or dividends, it wouldn't have been net worth.

That money was tied up in the $30 million that our clients owed us at the time. At that point in our operation, our clients owed us between $30 and $40 million total at any given time. Because we had a net worth of $6 million, that was $6 million we didn't have to borrow for operating funds. That net worth allowed us to keep our line of credit lower than it would have been had we had a lower net worth.

This is basic business. You have receivables on your books that you will collect in the future; that's an asset. Let's say those receivables are $35 million; you know that money is going to come in, and you have a general idea of when. But you still have to go out next month and spend maybe $1 million in advertising to generate the $5 million to $6 million in sales that you need to continue the business. That very simple example doesn't consider the expenses involved in producing your product or service, such as materials, salaries, overhead, and so on—items that you have to pay for often long before you get paid by your customers. This is often why companies can't survive a period of rapid growth; even though sales are good, they don't always have the cash needed to pay their costs before they get paid by their customers.

It's easy to look at a balance sheet that shows—as ours did at the end of the first five years—$6 million of accumulated profits and think, hey, that company has $6 million in cash. But we didn't. Having that $6 million in cumulative profits meant we could tap our line of credit for less than we otherwise would have had we not retained the profits. Our line of credit was secured by our receivables, and our profit was in those receivables.

If you're having trouble understanding this, take a basic accounting class.

Speak the Language of Business

So many small businesses get into trouble because entrepreneurs often don't have a basic understanding of accounting, income statements and balance sheets. Accounting is the language of business and if you don't know how to speak it, you'll be limiting your business and financial growth forever.

> "Ask for what you want. Ask for help, ask for input, ask for advice and ideas—but never be afraid to ask."
> —Brian Tracy

For right-brained people, accounting is obvious. It's logical, and it makes perfect sense. But left-brained people, who tend to be creative, often struggle with these concepts and get into trouble when they don't understand the numbers.

I'm not suggesting that you need to be an accountant or a CPA to be a business success. In fact, many accountants don't have an entrepreneurial bone in their bodies. On the other hand, before he became a millionaire, John D. Rockefeller was trained as a bookkeeper. If you're going to be in business, you have to understand basic accounting—don't depend on someone else to understand and interpret the numbers for you.

Take Care of Your People

You may be the driving force behind your company, but your employees are what keeps you successful, so recognize and reward that. One great way to do that is by giving them an ownership stake in the company—that not only rewards them financially, it also motivates them to keep doing their best. But that's not enough. Think about all the things you hated when you were an employee and *don't do them* to the people who work for you. Think about all the things you said you'd do differently if you were the boss, and *do them*.

The term *your people* is not limited to your employees. It also includes your suppliers, your professional advisors, and anyone else who can have an impact on your operation. Apply the principle of reciprocation I explained in Strategy 5. When you treat your people right, they'll treat you right.

Knowledge Is Only Powerful When It's Shared

Be sure all the people on your team know what they need to know. Don't keep secrets from them. When we were raided by the IRS, one of the first things I did was let everybody know what was actually happening—separating the facts from the speculation—and that they would have jobs the next day. I needed them to have faith in me and the company so they could get back to work and be focused on serving our clients so that I, in turn, could focus on responding to the IRS raid.

In general, do my senior executives know more about what's going on in the company than the midlevel managers? Yes. And the midlevel managers know more than the entry-level workers. There will always be issues that require various degrees of confidentiality. But we don't keep secrets when there's no valid reason—we don't play "I know something you don't know" types of games.

When I was at Wikoff, I learned the value of personality assessments. I also learned there's a skill to interpreting the results of the personality assessments, and I wanted to learn how to do that. But my boss wouldn't let me. He was willing to share what the evaluations revealed about people—he was happy to say, "Here's how you deal with this guy, and here's how you deal with that guy." But he refused to allow me to take the week-long training program that would teach me how to do the analysis myself. He claimed it was a cost issue, but I believe it was really a power issue. He was the only person in the company, other than the owner, who knew how to interpret the tests. I think he believed that if he shared that knowledge with anyone else, it would dilute his power.

The company's owner rarely got involved in hiring anyone below the regional manager level, so my boss—being the only other person who could interpret the personality assessments—had the final say on whether or not to hire someone. The regional managers in the various manufacturing plants weren't allowed to make a final hiring decision without consulting with my boss about the candidates' personalities. He controlled the hiring of every single person in the company. It was a waste of executive time and talent.

It's OK to Not Know All the Answers
the First Time Around

I expect people to be prepared when they're working on projects and have reports due, or when we're having strategic planning sessions. But I also know that they will not always be able to answer all my questions the first time I ask, and that's OK. I'm an analyst. Give me a report on anything, and I'll have a hundred questions about it. And I know that chances are the person making the report won't be able to answer half of those questions when I ask. I let them know I understand that. But I expect them to find out and get back with me.

I don't need know-it-alls on my team. What I need are people who can find the answers to the questions I ask.

Another thing I do regularly is to ask a question, get the answer, and then ask why. Sometimes I already know the answer, but I ask it to see if they know and if they can explain it. If they don't know the answer or can't explain it, that tells me they're not looking at the right things in their area of responsibility. My questions aren't designed to be punitive, but to let all of us know what we need to work on so that the next time I ask, they'll have an answer that we'll both understand.

Never let people know what you'd *like* to hear when you ask a question because there's an excellent chance that that's exactly what they'll tell you. I know what my own thoughts, hopes, and wishes are—I don't need them reflected back at me when I'm looking for information. Be sure your people know it's safe to tell you something you may not want to hear.

Get Out of the Way

If you want your company to grow—whether in size or in profits or both—you've got to get good people on your team then get out of their way. The best way to identify those people is through

Never Allow Yourself to Be Held Hostage

As you achieve success, there will be people who want an unfair share of what you have accomplished. It might be an employee who develops an inflated perception of his self-worth. It might be an investor or a funding source who suddenly starts making unreasonable demands. It might be, as I shared in Strategy 2, a disgruntled former employee who makes unfounded charges or, as I shared in Strategy 4, a celebrity spokesperson who jacks up his fee because he thinks you can't afford to lose him.

Never be afraid to walk away from unreasonable demands—especially ultimatums. This is automatic for me. If you give me an ultimatum, you don't have to wait for my answer—it will always be that I'm not giving in, I'm not bowing down, and I'm not paying the ransom. In fact, if I have to, I'll pay more than the ransom to fight people who go for this type of blackmail.

If you let people know you're afraid of whatever the alternative to saying no to them is, you have no negotiating position. The first time you give in, you've announced that you're operating from a position of weakness and you've put the other person in a position of strength. They will use that strength to destroy you. You have to believe that no matter what people might be able to take from you materially, no one can destroy you without your cooperation. So don't cooperate.

Of course, you have to be prepared to accept whatever consequences come with your decision. Every time I've been in a situation where I was given an ultimatum, I was fully prepared for the consequences—and they weren't always pleasant or easy. I also took the time to learn from the situation, to figure out how things got to the point that such demands could be made, and to take steps to be sure such circumstances would never occur again. But I'm not going to let myself or my company ever be held hostage by anyone.

assessments, but regardless of how you end up doing it, you've got to get people on board who can do what you want, then you have to let them do it.

This is not always easy. After all, your business is your baby, and your natural inclination is going to be to stay involved in every aspect of it. And certainly you need to know what's going on. But force yourself to be a big-picture person, and let the people you hire do the jobs that you hired them to do.

History shows us that the best ideas come from the people doing the work, not the bosses. For example, Earle Dickson was a cotton buyer for Johnson & Johnson when he invented the Band-Aid bandage because his wife was often cutting her fingers with kitchen knives while preparing food. The first ballpoint pen was invented by Laszlo Biro, a Hungarian journalist, in 1938. Saran Wrap was accidentally discov-

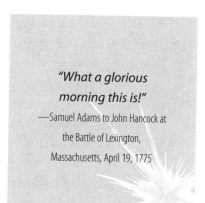

"What a glorious morning this is!"
—Samuel Adams to John Hancock at the Battle of Lexington, Massachusetts, April 19, 1775

ered in 1933 by Ralph Wiley, a college student who cleaned glassware in a Dow Chemical lab. American Airlines reportedly saved $40,000 in 1987 by removing one olive from each salad served in first class based on a suggestion from a flight attendant. At McDonald's, the Big Mac, Egg McMuffin, Filet-O-Fish, and Ronald McDonald were all developed by local franchisees, not the parent company. And speaking of McDonald's, it's interesting to note that in the 1950s, the franchisees often made more money than Ray Kroc, the company's founder.

My point is: Let your people do the jobs they were hired to do, and you'll likely be surprised and gratified by how much more they'll do than just their jobs.

Always Room for Improvement

No matter how good your operation is, you can always make it better. Be open to new ideas, new ways of doing things—especially when it comes to using technology.

When JK Harris & Company first started, we had one receptionist who took incoming calls and scheduled appointments. When the call volume got too heavy for her to handle alone, we added a second. Eventually, we had six receptionists who spent their entire day taking calls and scheduling appointments. They worked in the corporate office, where it's rare for us to have any visitors, so we don't need a traditional receptionist who greets people in person. They were scheduling one appointment for every three calls. We thought that was a decent ratio because we didn't know any better at the time.

That was in our early days when we were in our aggressive growth mode, opening new offices every week and staking our place as the industry leader. I needed a line of credit to fund this

Your Business Needs Good Habits

Brian Tracy, Steven Covey, and more all say you need to adopt the habits of successful people. This is true. Equally important is that your business needs to adopt the habits of successful businesses: delivering quality products and excellent service, operating efficiently and profitably, providing value for stakeholders, contributing to the community, and being an organization that's respected and emulated.

Take a look at the businesses you admire—the ones with loyal customers, happy employees, and soaring profits. What habits do those companies have that you could develop in your own operation?

growth. I found an angel investor in South Florida who said he was interested but that he had a policy of never investing in a business he didn't know at least a little about and could contribute something to in addition to money. But this was a new industry, and people didn't know much about it. I figured he was

> "The best and fastest way to learn a sport is to watch and imitate a champion."
> —Jean-Claude Killy

going to say no to the line of credit when he asked me, "How can I get involved in your business other than just providing money? What are your biggest headaches?"

I said, "Other than finding money?" We chuckled, then I decided I had nothing to lose by answering him. I told him that my biggest headache was dealing with the receptionists who handled the incoming calls in response to our ads. His eyes lit up, and he said, "I might have an idea. I'll get back to you in a couple of weeks."

This investor—his name was Ralph—had made his fortune in the vacation timeshare business, and I really didn't see a connection between that and tax representation. I went back to Charleston, and even though I didn't have much hope that he would lend me the money I needed, I followed up in two weeks and went back down to see him. (Another lesson: Always follow up when you say you will.) In that meeting were Bill, Ralph's accountant, and another guy, Joe, who had been the director of Ralph's call centers. Joe had lost his job when Ralph sold his timeshare business and had started a little call center in West Palm Beach. What I didn't know at the time was that Joe was struggling and needed business desperately, and Ralph wanted to help him and was willing to invest in his business as well as my business by putting us together.

Listen to the Experts

Ralph said he could give me a line of credit and take the appointment scheduling off my hands. Instead of taking the calls in my office in Charleston, we'd route them to Joe's call center in West Palm Beach, and we'd pay $35 for every appointment they scheduled.

I knew what it was costing us for each appointment, and it was more than $35. I didn't think Joe could make money at that rate, and I said so. I told Ralph I didn't want to get into business with someone who was going to have to renegotiate the deal a year later because they were losing money, but Ralph insisted that this was a win-win deal. When I asked him how it could be, he said, "Easy. We'll double your appointment volume." I couldn't believe it, because I thought our 33 percent appointment conversion rate was good. Ralph was only too happy to tell me it wasn't as good as I'd thought. He said, "In the timeshare business, we close one out of two, and the customer has to spend money right then. All *you're* asking people to do is come in, sit down, and talk to you. I guarantee we can get your appointment ratio to 60 or 70 percent." In three weeks, they got it to 80 percent—which just blew my mind because I thought we were doing the best we could do at 33 percent.

This taught me that sometimes experts know a lot more about particular parts of an industry than do the insiders. I knew absolutely nothing about call centers and timeshare selling. If anyone else had told me at the time that I could go to a call center and get those results, I would have thought they were crazy. But I needed Ralph's money, and I knew that he didn't get to be as rich as he was by doing stupid things. So I said yes to the deal, and it worked out great for all of us.

But I didn't just turn the call center part of our business over to Joe and forget about it. Within two years, I was an expert at running call centers. I knew every metric in the business—what the average time on the phone needed to be to make money, what an acceptable drop rate was, and so on.

Two years after we made that deal, we were looking for a permanent line of credit, and we were talking to some big financial institutions. They had a problem with our call center being owned by another company. That made sense, because even though I don't think Ralph and Joe would have ever done anything unethical, it was still possible that they could have held our business hostage because they owned the call center that was feeding all our appointments to our sales consultants. When I went to Ralph about this, he offered to sell me the call center for 10 percent of the stock in JK Harris & Company, so we did that deal with no cash exchanged at all.

Today, we schedule appointments from 83 percent of the incoming calls, and we do it with a staff of about 80 part-time people who work from their homes all over the country. They work 25 hours a week and make the same amount of money that we used to pay for someone to work a 40-hour week in our office—and they produce more. We don't have all the hassle and expense of maintaining a physical place for them to work, *and* we're getting better results.

Good Times vs. Bad Times

It's not hard to run a profitable company when the economy is expanding, but when times get tough, you can't absorb as many mistakes.

When times are good, the overall attitude of consumers is more positive, your profit margins will likely be higher, and you have natural expectations that the future will be better than the past. In bad times, it's just the opposite. Consumers develop a negative attitude, your profit margins shrink, and your expectations are that the future will be worse than the past. In that environment, you must operate your business differently.

In 2008, thanks to the recession and some other circumstances, things got bad for us. Cash was tight, and we weren't going to spend a penny we didn't have to. I told my executive team to come up with a plan to get us through the tough times, and that they could make whatever cuts they deemed necessary—nothing and nobody was off limits.

For example, we had a 78-year-old employee who was like a grandfather to everybody. He'd been with us for many, many years and was making a six-figure salary—but he just couldn't do the job anymore. We even had people handling his e-mail. But he was so beloved I was afraid of what it would do to morale if we forced him to retire. In good times, we were sufficiently profitable that we could absorb that expense, and that's what we chose to do. When times got bad, it became apparent that he had to retire. It was a tough decision, but we had to do it. People were sorry to see him go, but they understood.

> "An entrepreneur tends to bite off a little more than he can chew hoping he'll quickly learn how to chew it."
> —Roy Ash

Whether times are good or bad, I'm not going to keep anyone around who's hurting the company. But when I can afford it because times are good, I will opt for the kind, compassionate course of action over a strict dollars-and-cents approach.

Streamline and Centralize As Much As Possible

A certain amount of redundancy is important in any organization because you need backups. You don't, for example, want to have just one individual be the only person who knows how to do a key job. On the other hand, you don't need too many people doing the same job, either.

My brother, Bob, and his partner had been in the automobile business together since 1979. At that time, they had one dealership. By 1985, when I joined them as the corporate controller and a one-third partner, they had three dealerships: two in Georgetown and one in Conway, South Carolina. At that point, they were making less money with three dealerships than they had been with just one. While there were some market forces at work, a key reason for that was that each dealership was operating as an independent unit, so there was a tremendous amount of duplication, underutilization of resources, and inefficiency. The first thing I did was reorganize all three operations.

We set up a holding company and put the three dealerships under that. Then we created a management company and centralized all the accounting functions. I transferred the best of the office people to the management company and let four people go. The result was that the work was getting done more efficiently and at a lower cost.

It's easy for a growing organization to get fat. It's a lot like our bodies—you put on a pound or two, and you don't really notice it so you don't worry about it. You keep on eating those little extra goodies, and then you're up four or five pounds and you're starting to see it in how your clothes fit. By the time you hit 10 pounds, you're buying new clothes, but that's OK, you tell yourself, because you needed them anyway. And you keep gaining. A half a pound, a pound at a time, slowly, but still gaining. And then you wake up one morning and realize you're obese. And it's going to take a lot of dieting and exercise to get rid of that extra weight and get back to where you need to be, slim, strong, and healthy.

You'll see the same pattern in companies. Business is good, so you hire more people. Maybe you hire a few more than you need to, or you hire someone in a full-time position for a task that really only needs a part-time person, but that's OK because you're still growing, you figure that work is going to increase, everybody's doing well, and you don't realize you're starting to get fat. But then there's an economic downturn, or a new competitor comes on the scene and snags a significant portion of your market share, or fuel prices skyrocket resulting in an increase of virtually all your expenses—and suddenly you realize your company is obese. And if you want to survive, you need to slim down, and you need to do it fast. So rather than diet and exercise, you opt for surgery. But surgery has risks, and maybe it will go well, maybe it won't.

Prepare for Success

My point is that the best strategy is to avoid getting obese in the first place. Regularly review your operation for opportunities to streamline, consolidate, and centralize, and take those steps when they'll improve efficiency, productivity, and profitability.

However, just as you want to avoid becoming obese, you also don't want to get too skinny. There's a difference between "slim, strong, and healthy" and "lean and mean." Just the phrases themselves create two distinctly different pictures in your mind. There's value in having reserves to draw on if necessary, whether they're in the form of money, people, or other resources. You want to be efficient, but you don't want to cut so deep that you eliminate things you really need. Above all, consider your employees and your retention rate. Healthy companies enjoy a far lower turnover rate than unhealthy ones.

Lifetime Value of a Customer

The lifetime value of a customer is generally calculated by estimating the profit you anticipate from a customer over the period of time you expect that customer to do business with you. In tax resolution, our core business, the concept of the lifetime value of a customer doesn't apply. While our relationship with our customers typically exists over a long period because the tax resolution process takes so much time, it is actually just one transaction. We're a lot like criminal defense attorneys, where someone has what you hope is a one-time problem, you help them resolve it, and if all goes well, they'll never need you again. In the beginning, our attitude was we're never going to see these people again, so it really doesn't matter that much how we treat them.

I've learned a lot since then.

I've already talked about the importance of customer service to reduce complaints, because you may be doing everything right from a technical perspective, but if your customers feel they're not being treated with respect and consideration, they're not going to be happy and they're going to complain. If they can't get results by complaining to you, they'll go to an attorney, a regulatory agency, or a consumer reporter for help. This is an issue whether your customers make one-time or repeat purchases.

Another point to keep in mind is that people talk to each other about the companies they do business with. We get about 10 percent of our business in referrals. Though referral business isn't typically considered when calculating lifetime value, it's something to consider when you're tempted to give less than the best possible service. Satisfied customers will refer others to you. Dissatisfied customers will not only *not* refer others, they'll tell a lot of people how unhappy they were with your service—and the internet makes it easy for them to tell the world.

Every person on your team needs to understand the basic concept of the lifetime value of a customer. In his classic book, *Customers for Life: How to Turn That One-Time Buyer into a Lifetime Customer*, Carl Sewell wrote, "Every time you get a chance to sell a customer one item—be it a pack of gum or a car—you need to think about how much he represents in future business." That future business should include not only that customer's particular purchases but the business you might get from his referrals as well.

> *"Business opportunities are like buses, there's always another one coming."*
> —Richard Branson

While you may think your product or service is a one-time purchase, with some creativity, you may find you can add something else to your offering that will provide residual or at least some additional revenue. That's a major reason why I created our small-business services. Often the reason our business clients needed our tax resolution services was because they needed help getting their basic bookkeeping and accounting work done. By offering those services, we could keep them from being a repeat tax resolution client and create a long-term income stream for us. Once you have a customer—someone who knows you, likes you, and trusts you—look for ways to increase his value to your company.

Adding Services to Maximize Marketing Dollars

I'm a numbers guy, so I know what it costs to get a person to pick up the phone and call us. For the first couple of years, about half those calls were wasted money due to the fact that those people didn't qualify for our tax resolution services, usually because they made too much money or had too much in assets to be eligible for an offer in compromise. We'd just say, "Sorry, we can't help you, bye." But then they would ask us for advice on the best strategy to use to deal with their tax debt. We'd suggest they contact a financial planner who could analyze their situation and make an appropriate recommendation.

It bothered me that we had done a strong enough marketing job to get these people to call us, and then we were turning them away. Our sales consultants were complaining because they had nothing to sell these people. At the same time, I was trying to come up with ways to reduce our customer acquisition cost. The solution was to turn more of the calls into customers and that meant coming up with something that we could sell to the people who didn't qualify for our primary service. So we added financial planning services. If a client didn't qualify for our tax resolution service because of income or assets, the sales consultant could offer financial planning to help them decide the best way to handle getting the IRS paid. Now we had something to offer almost every person who walked through the door and sat down with a consultant, and we weren't wasting our marketing dollars.

Strive for Excellence

Do you remember *In Search of Excellence* by Thomas J. Peters and Robert H. Waterman? It's a business classic that should be required reading for anyone who aspires to own or even manage a business. It was first published in 1982, and it's still valid today.

It's true that some of the companies Peters and Waterman cite are no longer in business or may not qualify for excellent status today. That's one of the challenges of becoming excellent—you can't just do it and then stop working on it; it's an ongoing process. One of my earliest jobs was with an excellent company—Wikoff Color Corporation—and I spent nearly five years there as the corporate controller. Fred Wikoff intuitively knew and followed the principles Peters and Waterman articulated, and I was fortunate to have seen that in action at a young age. In fact, I had been working there for a year and a half before *In Search of Excellence* was published. When I read the book, I thought, this isn't new, Wikoff is already doing all this. But I also knew that the way Wikoff operated was special, not standard.

Peters and Waterman identified the eight basic principles top companies use to get to the top and stay there. Use them as a yardstick by which to measure your operation and to understand the operations of all the other players on your field.

1. A BIAS FOR ACTION

This is a preference for doing something—anything!—rather than sending a question through cycles of analyses and committee reports. Sometimes the action is wrong and you have some corrections to do, but in most cases, you're still ahead by having done *something* rather than nothing. When I started JK Harris & Company, I opened 400 offices in 40 states before I got my first business license. I explain how and why I did that in more detail in the bonus strategies, but the short version is that rather than take the time to figure out what each municipality I wanted to be in required and risk letting another company there get ahead of me, I took action. I got the offices opened and dealt with the consequences later.

I've never been afraid to take action, and I've never been content to sit and do nothing. I'm definitely an analyst, but I don't *over*-analyze—especially before trying something new. People on my team tell me that my willingness to explore and experiment is one of the main reasons working for JK Harris is never dull.

Here's another illustration of a bias for action. In August 1969, Sam Walton needed cash. He had 30 stores within 300 miles of the Bentonville distribution center, and his plan was to add at least 14 locations per year. But he didn't have the capital he needed to fund his ambitious expansion. This was, after all, long before Wal-Mart was a household name and Sam Walton was a legend. He had a $1.5 million line of credit with a Dallas bank, but he couldn't get them to let him draw on it, and he had a closing scheduled for the next day. That line of credit had been set up by Jim Jones, a banker Walton knew well and had worked with extensively. But Jones had left the Dallas bank to become president of the National Bank of Commerce in New Orleans.

With his back to the wall, literally needing the cash *that day*, Walton called Jones. Jones had promised the Dallas bank that he wouldn't take any business with him when he left, but he left the door open if a situation arose where the Dallas bank either fouled up or just didn't want the business. This situation fit the bill perfectly. Walton, who traveled in his own twin-engine Beechcraft Baron, had called Jones from Love Field in Dallas because he had been at the bank there trying to get a commitment for the cash he needed. Jones asked a few questions, made a decision, and took action. He told Walton to fly to New Orleans, where he was met by the bank's limousine and driven immediately downtown. It was a little after 6 P.M., and Jones had the paperwork ready for Walton's signature.

Walton got his money because both he and Jones had a bias for action.

A bias for action doesn't have to be only at the corporate level. Create a culture that pushes decision-making down to the lowest possible level in your organization. Bring the day-to-day decision making as close as you can to the people who are doing the day-to-day work. Set some guidelines so people understand how far they can go, then let them use their own judgment. Trust your people to make good decisions. As long as they're doing what they feel is best for the company and the customer, you can deal with any consequences if they make a mistake—but my experience has been that giving people clear guidelines along with responsibility and authority almost always produces positive results. Chances are, any mistake they might make won't be any worse than one their manager might make. A tremendous benefit of this approach is that you free up your managers and executives to focus on more strategic issues.

2. STAYING CLOSE TO THE CUSTOMER

Learn your customers' preferences, and cater to them. The one essential element no company can do without is customers, and if you don't stay close to them, you'll lose them. Wikoff Color demonstrated its mastery of this principle not only in the quality of its products but by being available to its customers on a 24/7 basis. Printers are not 9-to-5 operations, so Wikoff had people available at any time, day or night, if a customer called. Because of that, Wikoff customers were extremely loyal.

At JK Harris, we learned that lesson the hard way. A key aspect of staying close to your customer, especially in a service business, involves understanding and managing your customer's perceptions. There's a strong emotional aspect to the tax resolution business; being in debt to the IRS is a scary thing. Our advertising appeals to those strong emotions. But what we have to do after a client responds to the ad is to keep perceptions in line with reality, which is that we can't guarantee results and the process can take a long time. As I've mentioned before, in our early years, we focused on getting the work done and didn't concern ourselves too much with our customers' feelings, nor did we take the time to make sure their expectations were realistic. It was a big mistake.

Many of the challenges we had to overcome through the years could have been prevented had we stayed closer to our customers when we were the only show in town. Of course, we still face this challenge today. We have clients who walk out of their initial meeting with us thinking, "My IRS problems are over." No, they're not. The process of dealing with those problems is just starting and the client is responsible for doing a lot of work in terms of providing us with information and gathering documentation so we can do our job. Even though we tell them that and have them sign a document that clearly says it in bold type, we still have to work to manage their perception, which is often that because they've hired us, they don't have to do anything else and their tax problems are solved. Staying close to your customers and managing their expectations is always an ongoing challenge.

3. AUTONOMY AND ENTREPRENEURSHIP

This is demonstrated by breaking the corporation into small companies and encouraging them to think independently and competitively. If you're a smaller company, you can apply this strategy with departments. You'll get more creativity and more innovation out of small entrepreneurial units than you do out of massive corporate structures.

> "It makes you feel better about your own success if you don't just hoard all that money. I always pray to God, 'Well, give me enough to share and enough to spare.'"
>
> —Dolly Parton

At Wikoff, each plant was totally autonomous. They were even named to reflect that—they weren't just Wikoff Color, they were Wikoff Color Omaha, Wikoff Color Atlanta, Wikoff Color Jacksonville, etc. They all made the same products, but each plant manager was the leader of his small, 10- to 20-employee company that had its own asset allocation, profit and loss statement, and balance sheet. Each plant had the freedom to innovate, and when one came up with an idea that worked, it was adopted by the others. The reason they were so creative was because they weren't being told how to do things; they knew they had to produce certain results, and they were free to find the best way to do it.

At JK Harris, the person in charge of each business unit has full autonomy to run his or her own show, as do the regional managers. And within the various business units, the workers are broken down into small teams of eight to ten people at the most who specialize in various functions. They're free to figure out the best way to do their jobs, and when they come up with a good idea, we spread it to the other teams. They do, however, work within a structure to avoid communication and service problems. We want autonomy and entrepreneurial thinking—not anarchy.

4. PRODUCTIVITY THROUGH PEOPLE

Create in all employees the awareness that their best efforts are essential and that they will share in the rewards of the company's success. Build an environment where people doing their absolute best is routine and where workers have a vested interest in the organization's overall success. When I started JK Harris, I set aside 40 percent of the company's equity in an employee trust, so that's there for the employees' futures. We also pay productivity bonuses to every employee in the company—every single one of them has the potential to earn more than their base salary.

Our bonus system gives employees individual goals for their own compensation that clearly tie into the larger goals of the company. As performance continues to improve, profitability increases, and with that come the resources to reinvest in the organization to generate new ideas and additional growth.

Something we've learned about productivity bonuses is that it's important to make sure that they're based on team as well as on individual performance. Don't create a system that encourages people to neglect the company's mission or their team in pursuit of their own personal reward—or even worse, motivates them to start picking and choosing where they'll focus their efforts based on whether or not they'll get a bonus for it.

5. HANDS-ON, VALUE-DRIVEN

Insist that your executives keep in touch with the firm's essential business. Don't allow your senior people to develop executive suite isolation or be distracted by nonessentials. Our executives work where their people are, not in the "executive wing." In fact, our executive vice president of sales and marketing works from his home in Arkansas instead of from the corporate office in Charleston because he stays on the road with the regional managers and sales consultants most of the time. When my brother, Bob, became vice president of operations, he moved his office to be in the center of the action. He sits in the middle of operations, and so does Josh Baker, our vice president of client advocacy. Make sure your executives don't lose touch with the people who are actually doing the work.

6. STICK TO THE KNITTING

Remain with the business the company knows best. Certainly there's value to diversification and product line expansion, but it has to make sense. There are very sound business reasons for companies to add to their product and service lines, and you can do that while you still "stick to your knitting." Our prospective clients have to meet certain requirements to qualify for our tax resolution services. For example, they can't have excessive liquid assets that can be sold to meet their IRS obligation—if they do, the IRS expects them to sell those assets and pay up. If they have the ability to pay their taxes, even though it might mean selling some liquid assets or setting up a payment schedule, the IRS won't accept an offer in compromise (which is when the taxpayer or his representative reaches an agreement with the IRS to settle a tax liability for less than the full amount owed). So people in those circumstances would respond to our ads, but we couldn't help them because they didn't qualify. However, when we would explain that to them, they would often ask for advice on which asset to liquidate to pay their tax liability. To address this market, I created JK Harris Advisors, which is a fee-based financial planning service. We do the analysis, create a tax and financial plan, and then the clients use their own choice of professionals to implement the plan. JK Harris Small Business Services was created for a similar reason. As I've already mentioned, the reason many small-business owners get into tax trouble is because they don't have the internal resources to efficiently handle tasks such as accounting, bookkeeping, and tax preparation. Again, we can't provide tax resolution services if they have the resources to pay their taxes, but we can provide accounting-related business services to help them get and stay current on their tax obligation. It wouldn't make sense to offer services totally unrelated to taxes and accounting. We do what we know and what our clients know us for doing.

That's what you call good diversity. A few years ago, I did something that was bad diversity. Actually, it was horrible—a big mistake that cost us about $6 million. I got involved with a couple of construction businesses. It seemed like a good idea because I had construction experience. My plan was to use JK Harris to fund those companies and then later personally buy them from the corporation. But it diverted my attention and then the real estate market crashed—and so did the construction businesses. As I watched the money disappear, I realized I should have stuck to my knitting.

7. SIMPLE FORM, LEAN STAFF

Have few administrative layers and a small number of people at the upper levels. Don't get bulky with a lot of people doing things that don't need to be done. Wikoff Color was a great example of this. Fred Wikoff kept his corporate structure flat and lean. He was at the top, with one person unofficially between him and the plant managers.

In the largest organizations, you shouldn't have more than four levels between the CEO and the lowest ranking person in the company. In our sales group, we have exactly four levels: there's me, the executive vice president of sales and marketing, the regional managers, and the sales consultants. In our operations, there's me, the executive vice president of operations, the manager/supervisors, and the production employees who do the work. That's hard for some companies to do, but it's worth the restructuring effort to stay simple.

If you allow it employees will build fiefdoms. They'll get a bunch of people working for them that they don't really need and you'll end up with a massive bureaucracy that you can't control.

When it comes to your structure, focus less on how things look on paper and more on how they're actually working.

8. SIMULTANEOUS LOOSE-TIGHT PROPERTIES

Foster a climate where there's dedication to the central values of the company combined with tolerance for all employees who accept those values. At JK Harris, we're all on the same team, but we also celebrate individuality. The only place our people march in lockstep is in their commitment to serving the customer with professionalism, courtesy, and integrity. Be sure your people are allowed to let their individuality and creativity show through in their work. That's where you'll get improvements in your operations, processes, procedures, and systems. You need to have tight controls, but people still need enough freedom so they don't feel like they're in a prison.

> "Avoid having your ego so close to your position that when your position fails, your ego goes with it."
> —Colin Powell

Given a Choice, People Prefer to Do a Good Job

Alex Hiam, who provides leadership development and training to major corporations, recommends creating a culture that doesn't force people to do bad work. In *Making Horses Drink: How to Lead and Succeed in Business*, he writes: "Motivation expert Dean Spitzer points out that employees want to do a good job. Pride in a job well done is one of the most powerful motivators. But too often, we design or manage the work so as to make it impossible to do an excellent job. This sets up a basic disconnect for employees that leads to frustration and early burnout. For instance, if you insist that employees handle customer calls quickly, you may be forcing them to brush off complaints instead of resolving them properly. (I'm convinced that red-tape barriers to doing a good job are a *major* cause of poor attitudes and resignation letters. This is a good issue for any leader to work on.)"

Failure Is OK

Even as you work to create an excellent company, you also want to build an environment where it's safe to fail. In too many companies, one mistake means you've lost your job. And certainly there are some things for which immediate termination is appropriate, such as theft and violence. But when people are afraid to make mistakes, the organization becomes dull and stagnant. You don't want people keeping great ideas to themselves because they aren't sure if they'll work. You want them to feel safe trying new things so that you don't miss out on the ideas that will have a positive impact on your operation.

Danish physicist Niels Bohr said, "An expert is a person who had made all the mistakes that can be made in a very narrow field." In *How We Decide*, Jonah Lehrer writes: "Expertise is simply the wisdom that emerges from cellular error. Mistakes aren't things to be discouraged. On the contrary, they should be cultivated and carefully investigated." The human brain learns from mistakes, so when you have people who are making mistakes, they're getting smarter—and you can benefit from that.

In every business I've ever owned or managed, I've tried to create an environment where people know it's safe to fail. The people who are actually doing the work are going to be your best source of ideas, and you don't want to stifle them. At JK Harris & Company, we've done so many things that have never been done before.

> *As you go the way of life, you'll see a great chasm. Jump. It's not as wide as you think.*
> —Native American Proverb

Because we didn't have models to follow, we had to experiment—we had no choice. Some of those experiments didn't work, but we figured things out as we went along. We put teams together to come up with new ideas. When a team had something they had worked on and refined, we tested it on a small scale before we rolled it out to the entire company. (I explained this in Strategy 1.)

We've set up reward and recognition systems to encourage ideas on ways to do things better, to save money, to improve customer service. Equally important is that we don't punish people who come up with ideas that don't work. They don't get a reward, of course, but they are praised and recognized for trying.

Bottoms Up

A great way to encourage creativity and innovation is to get everybody—even the lowest person in the company hierarchy—involved in making the company better. When we were top-down driven, we were doing OK, but things weren't great, and I was constantly frustrated by the struggle to make things better. But when we started driving change from the bottom up, that's when things started to come together, people really got involved, and the ideas and suggestions started flowing at a phenomenal rate. The best systems we've ever come up with were developed by our employees.

Winners, Losers, and the State of Excellence

A key difference between winners and losers in business is that winners are constantly trying new things, making mistakes, and fixing them. If your objective is to get your company as close to perfect as you can, you're going to need to make regular corrections—and that means frequent changes.

Being an excellent company is an ongoing process. What made you excellent last year may not accomplish that goal today. You're not going to get it right and have it stay right. Something will change and you'll have to change because of it.

Will you ever reach that perfect state of excellence? Maybe. Maybe not. But try anyway. Losers don't bother to try because they figure you'll never achieve such a high goal. Winners are constantly trying to make their business better than it was the day before.

So do it, fix it, then do it again.

─── **KEY LESSONS** ───

✳ *To manage a successful business, you must be prepared for success.*

✳ *Healthy, financially stable, profitable companies have the resources to contribute to overall economic growth, create jobs, and make a positive impact on their communities.* The way to become such a company is to plan for it from the beginning.

✳ *The faster you grow, the more cash you will need to fund your growth.* Do solid cash-flow calculations so you know what you're going to need and can secure the funding in ample time.

Develop and maintain strong relationships with your lenders; treat them like they're partners in your business, because in many respects, they are.

※ *Consider how big you really want to get.* Growth is an admirable goal, but it's not always the best goal. Think about your position in the marketplace and plan an appropriate growth strategy.

※ *No matter how successful your company gets, don't stop learning.* You'll always need to know more than you do.

※ *Develop an understanding of basic accounting.* If you're not good with numbers or don't understand financial reports, take a class and learn.

※ *Take care of the people who are helping you succeed.* This includes your employees, advisors, suppliers, and anyone else who's supporting your efforts. Treat them with respect, compensate them fairly, and reward them in meaningful ways.

※ *Don't keep what you know to yourself.* Shared knowledge is infinitely more powerful than information kept secret.

※ *It's OK if people can't answer you immediately as long as they can find the answer to your questions.* When you get an answer, ask for the logic and explanation behind it.

※ *Never give in to unreasonable demands or business blackmail.* Don't allow yourself to be held hostage by threats or ultimatums.

※ *Put good people in the right positions, make sure they're trained, then step aside and let them do their jobs.*

※ *No matter how well you're doing, there is always room to improve.* Be open to new ideas that might make your good company even better.

※ *Develop good habits for your business.*

* *Listen to the experts.* Don't follow their advice blindly, of course, but respect their expertise, especially in areas where you're not as familiar.

* *Recognize that you'll probably operate differently when the economy is expanding than you do when it's contracting.* When times are tough, you don't have the margin to absorb as many mistakes.

* *Constantly monitor and evaluate to keep your operation as efficient as possible.* Inefficiencies and corporate "fat" increase gradually, and you may not notice you're "gaining weight" until you're bloated. Conduct regular reviews looking for opportunities to streamline, consolidate, and centralize your operations to keep efficiency, productivity, and profitability at its highest level.

* *Recognize the lifetime value of a customer.* See beyond a single transaction and consider how much a customer will spend with you over a lifetime. Also consider the value of the referrals a customer might make.

* *If people who aren't in your target market are responding to your marketing efforts, figure out what they're looking for, find a way to expand your product line, and provide the solution.* Don't let those marketing dollars go to waste.

* *Make excellence an ongoing goal.* The principles of excellent companies as outlined in the classic business book *In Search of Excellence* are as valid today as they were when that book was first published in 1982. Those principles are: a bias for action; staying close to the customer; autonomy and entrepreneurship; productivity through people; hands-on, value-driven; stick to the knitting; simple form, lean staff; and simultaneous loose-tight properties.

* *Mistakes happen.* You'll make them, and your people will make them. Build an environment where people know it's OK to try

new things, even if some of their ideas might turn out to be mistakes.

★ *It's OK to fail.* All successful people have a long list of failures in their history. Don't punish yourself or others for failing. Learn from it, and move on.

★ *Take a bottoms-up approach to improving your operation.* The people who are on the front lines usually have the best ideas for making things better.

Wait, There's More! Bonus Strategies

The seven strategies in this book are indeed critical to winning in business, and it would be nice if that were all you needed to know—but wait (as they say in television infomercials), there's more!

This section is your bonus, and you don't have to pay extra for it. These are things I've learned along the way that I've found valuable, and I think you will, too. So, in no particular order, let's begin.

Be in the People Business

Whatever your product or service is, be in the people business first. Identify every point of contact with your clients, and make that contact as easy and customer-friendly as possible.

Give Back

I'm a big believer in giving back, and entrepreneurs are fortunate enough to be able to do it in two significant ways. One is by giving some of our own money to charities and civic efforts. The other is by creating jobs, which not only boosts the overall economy but also provides income to people who can then contribute part of their money to charities and civic efforts.

My own personal preference is to do my charitable giving anonymously. I don't do it for recognition. You're never going to see a building or a plaque or whatever with my name on it. At the same time, I recognize that it's important for people to know that many wealthy people are generous givers. So do your giving in whatever way makes you comfortable—but do it.

Get Your Spouse on Board

I have always known my life was going to be an incredible adventure. While I was still in school, I made up my mind that I wasn't going to live a boring life, that I would take risks, and that I was willing to accept the possibility of economic extremes rather than consistent mediocrity. When you take risks, sometimes you win, and sometimes you lose. And I have gone from broke to millionaire and back to broke three times.

My wife knew what I was like before she married me more than 30 years ago, and she was willing to go on the adventure with me. If you want a life of entrepreneurial adventure *and* you want to be married, you need a mate who's willing to take that roller coaster ride with you.

Understand Cycles

We have to understand that the world and life and business is cyclical. You ride the waves up, and you ride the waves down.

Sometimes you don't survive the ride down. But that's OK, because there will always be another wave you can get on for the ride back up. And at least you're out there riding the waves, not sitting in a dull, boring job waiting to get laid off.

> *"If you're looking for a big opportunity, seek out a big problem."*
> —Unknown

Know When to Break the Rules

Sometimes you have to break some rules. I'm not talking about bucking traditions or doing things differently. I'm talking about serious rule-breaking with potentially serious consequences.

When I was opening our first 400 offices, we leased space in executive suite facilities, which allowed us to be up and running almost immediately with a minimum amount of capital investment. I'd choose our next city, rent an office in an executive suite, assign a sales consultant to the territory, place an ad in the paper, and we were in business. But I knew that in every single one of those cities, I needed a business license. I also knew I needed to register with the secretary of state in each state where we wanted to do business.

It would have taken at least one full-time person to handle all those licenses and registrations, and it would have slowed down our expansion. I knew that because when I first started, I tried to obtain all the licenses and permits before opening the first few offices, but I couldn't deal with the delays. I gave it some serious thought. I asked myself if I was going to let a bunch of government bureaucrats determine whether or not I could be in business for myself, whether or not I could grow my business according to my plan, and whether or not I could help the people who needed the services I was offering. I decided no, I wasn't going to let bureaucrats make these decisions for me and my company. I was going to do it myself.

So I didn't bother to obtain a business license or register with the secretary of state until we had been in business a couple of years—and I paid a price for it. It cost about $250,000 to $300,000 in fines and penalties. But if I had gotten the licenses as we went along, it would have cost me more than $50,000 a year to have someone on staff to handle the process. More important than that, though, is that the ultimate cost of delaying the opening of each office would have been astronomical. I estimated that it would have taken me two months on average just to get the legal clearance to open each office—and I was opening 12 offices a month, and getting each one of them going in just a couple of days each.

I made the decision that during the expansion phase of the business we wouldn't register our company or license our offices in the various states and municipalities where we were located. We would wait until we had all of the offices opened, then we would hire a full-time administrative employee to do nothing but take care of getting each office registered and licensed in the 40 states and 400 municipalities in which we operate. And when we hired that person, she had her hands full for the first year! But she got us in compliance, and we have stayed that way ever since.

What Are the Consequences?

Failing to get a business license is a simple civil issue subject to fines and penalties at most. It's not a criminal issue. So when I looked at the consequences of not getting the licenses and permits and compared that against the consequences of slowing down my growth and giving my competitors a heads up about what I was doing, it was a no-brainer. Another point I considered was that we had competitors who were advertising in multiple states, but they just had one office. They were only registered and licensed in the state where they were physically located, but they had clients in multiple states because they were selling by phone. I was willing to make the financial investment in physical offices across the country as well as in people so I could give my clients better service. But in doing that, I was giving my competition an advantage because I needed business licenses and permits that they didn't. It didn't seem fair or even sensible to me, so I decided not to let 400 different municipal governments be a roadblock to my success. I knew it would cost me, but it was money well-spent. I considered it simply a cost of doing business.

So yes, I broke the licensing and registration rules, but it was worth it. Business history is full of successful people who have bent and broken the rules, and we've seen a bunch of them go to jail. I have absolutely no tolerance or compassion for anyone who acts out of selfishness and greed, and whose conduct harms innocent people. But I do understand why people sometimes make the choices they do.

In 1975, FedEx founder Fred Smith was indicted for using a forged document to obtain a $2 million bank loan. In a press statement, Smith said, "I scraped up and borrowed every nickel I could. In February 1973 while attempting to raise the money from our current institutional investors and our banks, Federal Express needed additional money to survive. Accordingly, I borrowed a large sum of money from a Little Rock bank using a buy-back agreement of my stock in the family company. . . . the U.S. grand jury in Little Rock . . . returned an indictment alleging that I improperly prepared the documents involving the family company to secure the loan from the Little Rock Bank. . . . Although it would be improper for me to further comment on the merits of this case while it is before the court, I know my intentions were absolutely correct and am confident that this complicated matter will be decided favorably."

In court, Smith admitted to submitting a document that recorded a meeting that never actually took place to secure the loan. He said, "I submitted to the bank a resolution of the

Frederick Smith Enterprise Company of a buy-back, which I fully believed that I had." When the prosecutor asked if the document was "false and fictitious," Smith answered, "If you're saying that the meeting never took place, that's correct, and if you're saying that I signed Bobby Cox's name, that's also correct." When questioned again about the document being "false and fictitious," Smith said, "Well, to my own mind, no, sir, because that buy-back existed, and it exists to this day." Later in his testimony, he conceded that the document did not represent an actual meeting of the company but repeated that the buy-back existed and that the prosecutor hadn't proved that it didn't.

Smith was acquitted. It certainly wasn't the end of his professional and personal challenges, but it did mark a turning point in the company's history.

Smith clearly did something wrong when he prepared the documentation for the bank. Though he believed that the document represented the truth in terms of the resources to secure the loan, the document itself was false, and that's fraud. As it happened, Federal Express became profitable, was able to repay the loan, and the bank never had to rely on the collateral, so no one lost money on the deal. And chances are, no one would have ever even known about this if one of Smith's sisters hadn't filed a civil suit against him claiming his mismanagement of the family trust, which is what led to the investigation.

My point in sharing this story is that it's not unusual for entrepreneurs in difficult situations to not only push the envelope but to actually cross the line in their efforts to keep their companies alive and profitable. If nobody gets hurt or blows the whistle, they aren't likely to get caught. But is it worth the risk of losing everything and going to jail? For me, it's not. When I made the choice to open my offices without proper licenses, I knew it was a civil issue that would only result in fines. I wasn't risking anything but my own money.

When I Said No

After I closed my mechanical contracting business, I decided to get back into the automobile business. I moved to Florida for a few years, then had the opportunity to return to Charleston to work as the general sales manager for an Infiniti dealership. Six weeks later, I was unemployed.

The second week I was there, I went to the owner and suggested we do some direct mail advertising because that had worked well for me before. He refused and told me to just stick with newspaper ads. A few weeks later, the bookkeeper walked into my office, tossed a form she had prepared on my desk, and told me to sign it. I don't sign anything if I don't know what it is, so I started asking questions.

She finally explained that the form was the dealership's reimbursement request for co-op advertising. The way it worked with the luxury imports at the time was that the manufacturers set a goal for dealers to spend in advertising each quarter and agreed to match the amount at typically 75 or 100 percent. If the dealer spent the designated amount, he got the matching funds. If the dealer missed the goal by even $1, there was no match. Period. The form had to be signed by the general sales manager, not the dealer's principal. The logic behind that was that if the dealer was going to commit fraud, he would have to bring the general sales manager into the fraud with him.

The form said we had spent $40,000 in direct mail advertising, and I knew we hadn't—in fact, the owner had told me he didn't think direct mail was effective. So I went to the owner and asked him about it. He told me to just sign the form (although not in such simple language—he used some rather choice adjectives). I repeated that I wanted to know where the money went, and he again told me to just sign. I said no, that I thought he was committing fraud, and he could sign the form himself.

He fired me on the spot.

> *"A large portion of success is derived from flexibility. It is all very well to have principles, rules of behavior concerning right and wrong. But it is quite as essential to know when to forget as when to use them."*
>
> —Alice Foote MacDougall

I was fine with that, because I was ready to quit over being asked to sign the fraudulent form anyway. I wasn't going to commit a crime for anyone. Moreover, I don't steal; it's wrong. And I didn't want to work for someone who thought it was OK. I later found out that the dealership owner and the factory rep that serviced his account "owned" the company that generated the direct mail invoice, and they were stealing the co-op advertising money from the manufacturer. It was common practice in the industry at the time; and, although a few dealers had been caught and prosecuted, it obviously was still going on. That was when I decided I'd had enough of the car business, and I opened my accounting practice.

When you're facing something like this, do the same thing I did: Determine what the consequences are of following the rules and what the consequences are of breaking them. I was willing to accept the consequences of opening offices without getting the proper licenses ahead of time; I wasn't willing to accept the consequences—both from a legal standpoint and from the perspective of having to live with myself—of stealing. So give the situation however much thought you need to, then do what's best for your conscience and your business.

Look at the Dark Side

I'm a firm believer in the value of a positive attitude. I believe when you expect the best, you generally get it. But it's also a good idea to have a devil's advocate who's available to look at the possible negatives whenever you're planning something to make sure you're seeing everything clearly. The goal is not to stop you from taking any particular action but to be sure you're prepared for all the contingencies when you do.

Stay Calm and Don't Panic

When unexpected things happen, don't panic. Remember that your employees, customers, and suppliers are looking to you for guidance and leadership. You can't make good decisions when you're panicking. Take the time to collect your thoughts and respond with logic and reason—don't indulge in knee-jerk reactions.

When the I-35 bridge over the Mississippi River in Minneapolis collapsed during rush hour on August 1, 2007, dozens of cars and their occupants plunged into the water, and 13 people died. Assistant Fire Chief John Freutel's calm, systematic action likely significantly reduced the number of fatalities. In an interview, Freutel said, "There isn't a manual on how to deal with a bridge collapse. I was juggling 10 million things, but 30 years of experience helped me stay calm. When you're in command, I've learned the most important lesson is: Take a deep breath."

You probably won't ever have to deal with anything so dramatic, but you'll have to deal with plenty of things you weren't anticipating. Stay in control by staying calm.

Dealing with Obstacles: Go Around, Over, or Through, but Don't Stop

Business is a lot like climbing a mountain that has a lot of milestones but no summit. Sometimes the path is smooth, sometimes it's rocky, and sometimes it's completely blocked by a boulder.

My personal philosophy is that nothing—not any person, any thing, or any circumstance—will stand in the way of my success. Let me be clear here that I'm not advocating operating in any way other than honestly and ethically. What I'm saying is that when something gets in my way, I don't just give up, I figure out a way to deal with it so I can keep moving toward my goals.

There's a great story about Larry Ellison in Mike Wilson's book *The Difference between God and Larry Ellison* that illustrates how winners deal with obstacles. Bruce Scott was Oracle's first employee, after the two software development founders (Ellison still hadn't left his "day job"). Wilson writes:

> *Bruce Scott's first experience with Larry Ellison was an eye-opener. On one of his first days at SDL [which became Oracle], Scott was trying to connect SDL's computer terminals to the Precision Instrument computer. There was a problem: A Sheetrock wall stood between the SDL offices and the [Precision Instrument] computer room. Scott said, "Larry, we need to hook up these terminals. How are we going to hook them up?" "I'll show you how," Ellison replied. He grabbed a hammer and smashed a hole through the wall. Bruce Scott came to believe that Ellison's entire business philosophy could be summed up in that single act. "Find a way or make one. Just do it," Scott said.*

I've done the same thing when we needed something—more room or people or money or whatever. Most of the "walls" that you'll encounter in business are rarely more than drywall that you can smash through and repair.

In Ted Turner's book, *Call Me Ted,* John Malone, chairman of Liberty Media Corporation, shares this observation about Turner:

> *Ted asks himself the question, "If a rule doesn't let me do something that's so logical, it must be a bad rule. And if it's a bad rule I ought to be able to change it or it should just go away." He's always had that kind of basic, almost childish, logic about him that refuses to accept artificial impediments. I think one of his big secrets of success over the years is that the things that most of us would sit there and ponder—all those regulatory and legal reasons*

why it might not be something you could do—Ted would just say, "Oh, hell, you can overcome those kinds of things," and he'd just go do it.

There are times in business when being childish pays off, when you need to look at things in a simple, logical, uncomplicated way and figure out how to get what you want accomplished. Don't allow yourself to be blocked by barriers that you can easily circumvent.

The Age-Old Pricing Dilemma

You don't have to be the lowest priced provider in the marketplace. When I was at Wikoff Color, our prices were about 15 percent higher than most of our competitors, and we had enough business to keep more than 20 manufacturing plants going across the country. The reason customers were willing to pay the premium was because we made a superior product, and we backed it up with unmatched service.

The printing ink Wikoff made was used to print the boxes for food packaging—cereal, crackers, cookies, cake mixes, etc.—and quality and consistency are absolutely critical. Think about it: If you're in the grocery store and you pick up a box of your favorite breakfast cereal and you notice that the color on the package looks a little faded or just not quite right for some reason, or the shade on one package is different from the one next to it, you sub-consciously question whether there's something wrong with the contents. On an intellectual level, you know that the exterior pack-age has absolutely nothing to do with the contents, but on an emotional level, you can't help but wonder. Consumers don't want to buy those not-quite-right colored packages, so printing ink quality is critical.

Printers generally run 24-hour operations, which means they may have issues for their suppliers in the middle of the night.

Wait, There's More! Bonus Strategies   **201**

Many suppliers say, "You've just got to wait until we open in the morning." Wikoff didn't. If a printer set up a press with Wikoff ink, did a test, and the blue or the orange or whatever didn't look right, the press operator could call Wikoff at any time of the day or night, and someone would be dispatched to the customer's site immediately to remix the ink or do whatever it took to correct the problem. In most cases, we could have a technician on the customer's site within a half an hour of the call, so the printer didn't have to expend the labor to take down the job and put up another until the problem could be resolved.

> "Remember not only to say the right thing in the right place, but far more difficult still, to leave unsaid the wrong thing at the tempting moment."
>
> —Benjamin Franklin

For Wikoff customers, that level of service was well worth paying a 15 percent premium. After all, it saved them from expensive downtime. Customers, whether they're individuals or businesses, will pay a premium for service that's important to them.

You don't have to be the least expensive to be a successful, profitable operation. As a matter of fact, if you try to be the cheapest in the market, you risk being perceived as cheap and low quality. This is especially important to keep in mind when you're selling services. There's a paradox about professional service fees—people often resent paying high fees or can't afford them, but they're also suspicious of the quality of a professional whose fees are substantially below the competition's. You walk a fine line in pricing in any type of service business.

Welcome Criticism

Effective leaders welcome criticism. Of course, you have to create an environment where people feel comfortable being candid with you, so don't shoot the messenger if you don't happen to agree with the message.

I look at criticism as that person's perception of me. If their perception is negative, I want to understand why. And then I can make a decision about how to deal with it. If I truly don't believe it's a real problem, I might just ignore it. Most of the time, though, I find criticism is an opportunity for self-improvement.

I used to be very careless with my language and used profanity pretty much all the time when I was in the office. After all, I had spent years in the construction and automobile businesses (where we were careful with what we said in front of customers, but it got pretty rough behind the scenes), so peppering my messages with four-letter words was a habit. Finally, one of my employees asked to speak to me privately. She was a very sweet, well-mannered lady who had been with me for quite a while. She did her job well, and I had a tremendous amount of respect for her.

We went to my office and closed the door. I had no idea what was on her mind, and I was shocked when she began speaking. She told me that my language made her and others in the office uncomfortable but more important, she said, was that I was making a poor impression on people who didn't know me. "I know where your heart is because I see what you do," she said, "but your language makes people think that your heart isn't like what I know it is."

That was a real eye-opener for me. She was exactly right. I was putting myself at a serious disadvantage when I was around people who were offended by profanity and who didn't know me well. I immediately cleaned up my vocabulary, and I'm very grateful to her for bringing the issue to my attention.

I could have gotten defensive. I could have told her it was my company, and I could talk any way I wanted, and if she didn't like it, she could leave. But instead, I did the smart thing. I listened to what she had to say, I evaluated the criticism on its merits, and I took appropriate action.

Get to the Root of Any Problem

When you've got a problem, don't just try to deal with the result—get to the cause. If you don't, you'll keep patching things up, but the problem will never get fixed.

Keep Pedaling

In *Everybody Wins: The Story and Lessons Behind RE/MAX*, authors Phil Harkins and Keith Hollihan write: "RE/MAX is not an ocean liner or a jet plane but a bicycle that they can never stop pedaling if they want to stay ahead of the pack." This is a great analogy for any business. Unlike ocean liners, you need to be able to make quick turns. And you can't fly on autopilot, like a jet plane. And while you might be able to coast for a very short time, you can't do it for long, because if you do, you'll get passed.

Don't Be a Hamster

> "Entrepreneurs are risk takers, willing to roll the dice with their money or reputation on the line in support of an idea or enterprise. They willingly assume responsibility for the success or failure of a venture and are answerable for all its facets."
>
> —Victor Kiam

While it's true that business is more like a bicycle than an ocean liner or a jet plane, it's important that your pedaling be getting you somewhere and that you give yourself regular breaks. When my daughter was young, she had a pet hamster. I used to watch that hamster run on his wheel, and I thought he was a classic example of so many American businesses: He would just run like hell, getting nowhere, until he gave out and collapsed.

I've met too many entrepreneurs over the years who function like a hamster. They run as hard as they can until they're exhausted, and when they stop, they're still in the same place.

If you're expending a lot of effort, make sure there's a worthwhile result. Run forward, not in place. And take a rest before you're so exhausted that you collapse.

Take Care of You

As a business owner or manager, you're going to spend a great deal of your time taking care of other people. Don't forget to take care of yourself. You are your most important asset, and you're not any good to anyone if you are sick and stressed out.

Protect your physical and emotional health. We all know to eat right, exercise, and get regular checkups, but we often find excuses to not do what we know we should. Dump the excuses. Find the discipline and the time to do what's best for you. Remember that your emotional health is every bit as important as your physical health. Stay in touch with your spiritual side, whether it's through prayer and meditation or some other means. Humans are emotional creatures with deep feelings, and it isn't practical or reasonable to expect that you can completely separate your feelings from your business. Don't even try.

If you have any reason to suspect that you may be suffering from any sort of mental health issue, even if it's "just" a mild case of depression, seek professional help. If you need counseling or even medication, get it. Don't sacrifice your peace of mind to any preconceived notions about the process or because of concerns about what people might think.

Put your family ahead of your business. Don't neglect your spouse; successful marriages take as much effort, if not more, as any business. You can always work, but your children will only be young once. Beyond your family, protect and preserve your friendships. All the business and financial success in the world

Wait, There's More! Bonus Strategies

will be meaningless if you don't have people you love to share it with.

Keep Going

Never surrender. Never give up. You may have to change your strategy. You may make mistakes and experience some failures along the way. Learn from them, and keep going.

Why Do You Do It?

What drove you to where you are today? Oracle founder Larry Ellison didn't have any great desire to be the leader in the software industry; he just didn't want to work for anyone else. "I think I was driven to do this because I knew I could not survive in a conventional corporation," he said. "I was not suited to being able to work my way up the corporate ladder." His business world experience was an extension of what it had been like for him in school. "If people asked me to do things that didn't make sense, I just couldn't do [them]. I couldn't start my own school, but I could start my own company."

The subtitle of Kim Kiyosaki's book, *Rich Woman*, is *Because I Hate Being Told What to Do*. In her introduction, she writes, "I knew I had a problem following orders even back in kindergarten! . . . The teacher said I was 'willful.' I just didn't like being told what to do. I was fired twice from my first full-time job out of college . . . I was just a bit too independent. . . . This issue was so ingrained in me that when someone would strongly tell me to do something, even though I knew it really would be best for me to do it, I wouldn't do it, just because I didn't want to be told what to do."

I totally relate to these statements, except my motivation was not only to be my own boss so that I didn't have to play corporate games and listen to people telling me what to do but to figure out how to keep from being bored. Once I master something and it's no longer a challenge, I get bored—and I don't like being bored. I think most entrepreneurs get bored quickly. I also think that true entrepreneurs are obsessed idiots, because they're not happy unless they're on the edge, taking risks. And they're always trying to figure out the next business.

As the CEO of my company, I make the decisions that set the direction of the company. Those decisions often involve doing things that present new challenges and fresh horizons, and that keeps things interesting for me and everyone in the organization. Also, as the CEO, I don't have to do anything that doesn't make sense to me. When I see things happening in the company that don't make sense, I question them. And I don't have to accept answers I don't understand.

I understand why I do what I do. Do you?

Now What?

You know what you need to do. Go do it—and then do it again.

Recommended Reading

When it comes to books, one is never enough. I encourage you to read at least one business book each week—more if you can. Let the experience and insight of others help you reach your goals quickly and efficiently. Here's a list of books that I have relied on as I have learned how to build and run successful businesses.

Brooks, Bill and Tom Travisano. *You're Working Too Hard to Make the Sale! More than 100 Insider Tools to Sell Faster and Easier*, Irwin

Brooks, William T. *The New Science of Selling and Persuasion: How Smart Companies and Great Salespeople Sell*, John Wiley & Sons

Cialdini, Robert B. Ph.D. *Influence: The Psychology of Persuasion*, William Morrow

Eichenbaum, David A. *The Business Rules: The Seven Irrefutable Laws That Determine All Business Success,* Entrepreneur Press

Gladwell, Malcolm. *Outliers: The Story of Success,* Brown and Company

Harkins, Phil and Keith Hollihan. *Everybody Wins: The Story and Lessons Behind RE/MAX,* John Wiley & Sons

Harpst, Gary. *Six Disciplines Execution Revolution: Solving the One Business Problem That Makes Solving All Other Problems Easier,* Six Disciplines Publishing

Hiam, Alexander. *Making Horses Drink: How to Lead and Succeed in Business,* Entrepreneur Media

Hogan, Kevin. *The Psychology of Persuasion: How to Persuade Others to Your Way of Thinking,* Pelican

Hogan, Kevin and James Speakman. *Covert Persuasion: Psychological Tactics and Tricks to Win the Game,* John Wiley & Sons

Keirsey, David. *Please Understand Me II: Temperment, Character, Intelligence,* Prometheus Nemesis Book Company

Lakhani, Dave. *Persuasion: The Art of Getting What You Want,* John Wiley & Sons

Lehrer, Jonah. *How We Decide,* Houghton Mifflin Harcourt

Lieberman, David J. Ph.D. *Get Anyone to Do Anything: Never Feel Powerless Again—with Psychological Secrets to Control and Influence Every Situation,* St. Martin's Press

Luntz, Frank. *Words That Work: It's Not What You Say, It's What People Hear,* Hyperion

Lynn, Jacquelyn. *The Entrepreneur's Almanac: Fundamentals, Facts and Figures You Need to Run and Grow Your Business,* Entrepreneur Press

Peters, Thomas J. and Robert A. Waterman. *In Search of Excellence*, Collins Business

Sewell, Carl. *Customers for Life: How to Turn That One-Time Buyer into a Lifetime Customer*, Broadway Business

Steinmetz, Lawrence L., Ph.D. and William T. Brooks. *How to Sell at Margins Higher than Your Competitors: Winning Every Sale at Full Price, Rate, or Fee*, John Wiley & Sons

Tracy, Brian. *Million Dollar Habits*, Entrepreneur Press

Trimble, Vance H. *Overnight Success: Federal Express and Frederick Smith, Its Renegade Creator*, Crown

Trimble, Vance H. *Sam Walton: The Inside Story of America's Richest Man*, Penguin Putnam

Turner, Ted. *Call Me Ted*, Grand Central Publishing

Welch, Jack. *Jack: Straight from the Gut*, Business Plus

Wilson, Mike. *The Difference between God and Larry Ellison*: Inside Oracle Corporation, *God Doesn't Think He's Larry Ellison*, Collins Business

About JK Harris

JK (John) Harris is the quintessential entrepreneur: an astute leader with tremendous business acumen who's always on the lookout for new opportunities. After holding senior management positions in a number of companies, he went on to found or purchase 18 businesses in his 30-year business career—and has plans for more.

The son of a schoolteacher and a federal government employee, John grew up on a dairy farm in rural South Carolina, which introduced him to a wide range of important business fundamentals at an early age. He attended Carlisle Military School in Bamberg, South Carolina, where he played basketball and baseball, developed his leadership skills, and graduated as salutatorian of his class. Continuing his education, he worked full time while attending the University of South Carolina, graduating *cum laude* with a degree in history and political science in 1976. He went on to earn his master's in accounting in 1977.

His first post-college job was as a staff accountant at Haskins & Sells, CPAs (now Deloitte Touche Tohmatsu) in Charlotte, North Carolina. During his 13 months with that firm, John achieved an important accomplishment and made a critical self-discovery: He received his CPA certificate and realized he was far better suited to being a CPA's client than a CPA. He launched his entrepreneurial career, and never looked back.

Over the years, he has been the founder, owner, or co-owner of businesses in a range of industries, including automotive and construction, as well as business, consumer, and professional services. He is, by his own admission, a serial entrepreneur. He's also easily bored, and that's what drives him to constantly seek new challenges.

John opened his accounting practice in 1996 to share his business expertise with other entrepreneurs in the Charleston area. When a new accounting client came to him owing the IRS $90,000, John was able to settle the debt for $42,000. In the process, he realized that there was a dearth of qualified assistance for taxpayers who were in debt to the IRS. He decided that JK Harris & Company would focus on those services and in 1997 decided to grow his two-person accounting practice into the nation's largest tax representation firm. In less than five years, JK Harris & Company went from a single office to 325 offices in 43 states with annual revenues of more than $100 million. Today, at 10 times the size of its nearest competitor, JK Harris & Company continues to lead the tax representation industry, and John continues to serve as president and CEO of the firm.

Crediting much of his success to lessons learned from other entrepreneurs as well as his own experience, John Harris has made it his mission to share his knowledge and expertise with business owners and managers across the country and throughout the world through his books and speeches. In 2009, he created Flashpoints as a resource for entrepreneurs who want to grow bigger, stronger, more profitable companies. Visit theflashpoints.com for more information.

Index

Invite JK Harris to Speak at Your Event

JK (John) Harris is an engaging speaker with a valuable message about how you can take your business to the flashpoint of growth and profitability. John's dynamic presentations at conferences, conventions, and corporate meetings are designed to entertain, inform, and leave audiences energized, enthused, and looking forward to his next appearance.

JK Harris accepts a limited number of speaking engagements each year. To book him for your event, visit **www.theflashpoints.com** today.

Take Your Sales Team to the Flashpoint!

To attain the pinnacle of sales achievement, companies must hire the right salespeople, train those salespeople well, and manage them effectively. Any one of these efforts can produce positive, but still mediocre, results; put them together and you will reach the Flashpoint of sales.

The Sales Flashpoint: 15 Strategies for Rapid-Fire Sales Growth by JK Harris and Richard Dickerson tells you how to identify, hire, train, and coach a team of unbeatable sales superstars.

The Sales Flashpoint: 15 Strategies for Rapid-Fire Sales Growth is scheduled for publication in 2010.

To receive an e-mail alert letting you know when your copy will be available, visit

www.theflashpoints.com

flashpoints

Two Free Gifts for You from JK Harris

Thank you for reading *Flashpoint: Seven Core Strategies for Rapid-Fire Business Growth*. As an expression of his appreciation, JK Harris has two free gifts for you.

The first is JK Harris' exciting new e-book, *The Mindset of High Achievers*. Find out how high achievers think, how their mindset affects what they are able to accomplish, and how you can use the same techniques and strategies they do to achieve more with far less effort than you ever dreamed possible.

The second is a complimentary subscription to *Flashpoints* newsletter. Get JK Harris' wisdom and information delivered via e-mail. Each month, *Flashpoints* will bring you timely articles and resources to help you deal with issues related to starting and managing a fast-growing, profitable company—all absolutely free.

Help take your company to the Flashpoint by accepting these two free gifts from JK Harris. Visit **www.theflashpoints.com** to claim your gifts today.

flashpoints